THE
RAINBOW
ORACLE™

THE RAINBOW ORACLE™

TONY GROSSO
AND ROB MACGREGOR

BALLANTINE BOOKS • NEW YORK

Library of Congress Cataloging-in-Publication Data

Grosso, Tony.
    The rainbow oracle.

    1. Fortune-telling by colors.   I. MacGregor, Rob.
II. Title.
BF1891.C64G76   1989   133.3′3   87-91837
ISBN 0-345-35370-6

Book design by Alex Jay/Studio J
Manufactured in the United States of America
First Edition: June 1989

10 9 8 7 6 5 4 3 2 1

Acknowledgments

A special thanks to my sister, Amy, and her husband, Jack Chearmonte, who are an example of just how happy a relationship can be. To Philip, Rose, and Kathy Chearmonte for their enduring faith in me. To Joanne Ansell, Joseph Gehrlien, and Frank Webb for their friendship. And thanks to Diane Cleaver and Cheryl Woodruff for their special care.

—TG

A special thanks to Cheryl Woodruff, our editor and guiding light, who made it happen; and to agent Diane Cleaver for her perseverance.

—RM

CONTENTS

7

FOREWORD

IN THE MORE THAN TWEN-
ty years that I've worked as a psychic counselor, I've taught
numerous seminars and classes on how to develop intuitive
skills. Of the many methods I've used, color has not only
attracted the most interest, but has proven to be one of the
most effective devices in developing psychic abilities.

Color, of course, is an ever-present phenomenon of our
environment. At this moment, through my window, I can see
blue sky, white clouds, bright yellow sun, green trees, brown
earth, and orange and scarlet flowers. In fact, color is so much
a part of our lives that most of the time we only notice it at an
unconscious level.

But the hues of the rainbow are more than a reflection of
nature. Every color possesses meaning. For years, I painted as
a hobby and noticed that the colors in my paintings always
mirrored my moods. When my life was turbulent, the colors I
worked with were dark. When I was happy, they were bright
and cheerful. Today, I can still look back and tell exactly what
I was going through at a particular time in my life because of
the colors on the canvases.

Over the years, in my work as a psychic counselor, I

observed that people always wanted to learn how to do what I did—and yet how rarely they believed that they could do it. As for myself, I found it awkward trying to teach people about abilities that I regarded as a natural gift. Yet I still believed that everyone with an interest could be taught to develop their psychic talents. My challenge was to figure out how. I knew I needed a set of symbols that could trigger the unconscious and awaken each individual's latent psychic abilities— something that anyone could understand. The answer to my challenge to find an accessible tool for psychic development was both simple and profound—color!

After using color successfully in several psychic-development seminars, I began to realize that color was not only a valid teaching tool, it was also effective in my own psychic readings. I began experimenting with "color readings" and would ask clients to list several colors quickly off the top of their heads. Not only were the individual colors important, so was the order in which they were given. I positioned the colors the client presented using the Celtic Cross spread from the Tarot. This symbolic layout gave each color a framework for interpretation in both time and space—such as past and present positions, as well as obstacles and surrounding influences.

Soon I was refining my color divination system, working out the nuances in the meanings of the colors. After hundreds of color readings, I realized that certain color combinations possessed special meanings beyond their interpretations as individual colors and I incorporated this new information into my readings. Then, twelve years ago, I felt my system of color divination—tested in thousands of readings—was ready to be used as a tool for developing psychic awareness, and I self-published *Color Me Psychic*, a booklet describing my system and the divinatory meaning of colors.

I continued to use my color system in seminars. Among those who successfully learned my system and put it to use for themselves were many who had believed they didn't have any psychic talents. At last, they understood that all of us have psychic ability to varying degrees, and like any other skill, it's just a matter of developing and using it.

One of the most fascinating aspects of watching clients and students apply my color system was that often their logical minds got in the way. Once they became familiar with the meanings of colors, they wanted to pick the colors they thought were best for them. In order to bypass the demands of the ego, my color system evolved into the creation of color cubes and the *Rainbow Oracle*. Suddenly, those who knew the meanings of the colors were able to use the method without the interference of the intellect. Often, they were astonished by the results.

Since the meanings of the colors are my own, developed from trial and error over many years, they may differ from other interpretations you've read. But these are the ones that have worked for me and I'm confident they'll work for you as well.

★ ★ ★

I met Tony Grosso while working on a magazine assignment several years ago, and I was quite impressed by his method of using color in his psychic readings. Although I've had an interest in metaphysics for many years, I'd never associated color with the paranormal.

Tony explained that colors were a means of triggering the unconscious and made it easier for him to read a person. He assured me that anyone could use his method, and indeed with a little practice, you could become your own "psychic counselor." Before I left, he gave me a copy of *Color Me Psychic.* I looked the booklet over, filed it away, and didn't think much more about it.

Yet, from that point on, color began to play a much more important part in my daily life, particularly in my work as a writer. Suddenly, I was getting assignments where color played a key role. First, there was an article on the trend of color consultants for a business magazine. I wrote another on color and appearance for *Weight Watchers* magazine. The following year, I coauthored a book about "Miami Vice," the only TV series ever created with a mandatory color scheme. Over and over, behind-the-scenes people talked about the importance of the show's colors, a fact I emphasized in *The Making of Miami Vice.*

Meanwhile, I had begun experimenting with the idea that anyone could use color, as Tony suggested, as a divination tool. But I ran into a stumbling block. Because I knew the meanings of the colors, I discovered that my rational mind was interfering with my intuitive selections, nudging me to pick the colors I thought would give me the most favorable answer.

The question was, how could I get out of my own way? Tony and I discussed the question, and came up with the perfect solution—color cubes—a way to detach from the rational mind and let the intuitive mind take over.

As I began working with the cubes, keeping track of their answers, and using them with other people, I remembered what Tony had said years earlier and realized he was right. Color *is* a universal tool with which we can expand our world. I've found that color divination works equally well with people who are interested in the occult or in metaphysics and with those who are not. Belief and interest aren't prerequisites; the only things required are curiosity and an open mind.

Skeptics, such as the members of the Committee for the Scientific Investigation of Claims of the Paranormal (CSICOP), have said that the person receiving a reading is the worst one to judge its accuracy. The *Rainbow Oracle* is based on the opposite point of view, that individuals can think for themselves and judge what is real and what isn't.

You may begin your experimentation with the oracle because of an interest in color, because you want some guidance regarding a thorny dilemma, or just for fun. But whatever your reason, the *Rainbow Oracle* can serve as a remarkable tool that can allow you to take your life into a whole new dimension, in which color is the key to new levels of awareness and understanding of life's deeper meanings.

When we see a rainbow at the end of a storm, we think of hope, a promise of something to come. May the *Rainbow Oracle* guide you to the proverbial "pot of gold" that awaits you at the rainbow's end.

Tony Grosso
Rob MacGregor
Fort Lauderdale, Florida
June, 1989

"Paint rainbows in their hearts and minds."
Song of Heyoehkah
Hyemeyohsts Storm

"To one who views it with imagination, the whole rainbow manifests a streaming out of spirit and a disappearing of it again within. It is like a spiritual dance, in very deed a spiritual waltz, wonderful to behold."
—Rudolf Steiner

1
COLOR AS
ORACLE

EVERYONE KNOWS THAT seeing with two eyes is better than seeing with one. The world takes on greater dimension and depth. But, suppose you had the use of a third eye? Your perception of the world would be even deeper. Your inner self is like that third eye, and as you become attuned to it, your view of the world and of yourself broadens.

One means of opening the passageway between the inner self and the conscious mind is through the use of oracles. You may think of an oracle as a person—a medium or psychic—who looks into the future. In the history of Western culture, probably the best-known seer of this type was the oracle of Delphi in ancient Greece, where prophecies were delivered by priests and priestesses in response to earnest inquiries. In Greek mythology, Cassandra was an oracle who was destined always to speak the truth and always to be ignored.

You may also be aware of another type of oracle called "divinatory tools," which provide a symbolic system of coded information that can be cast and interpreted by the individual to shed light on any question imaginable. The most widely known of such tools used today are Tarot cards, Rune Stones, and the *I Ching*. These oracular systems, as well as others, have been passed on from ancient times.

HISTORY OF ORACLES

Bone oracles were used 5,000 years ago by a neolithic hunter-gatherer culture in China known as the Longshang. Their descendants, a Bronze Age people known as the Shang, divined the future by reading the cracks in tortoiseshells. This method was used by the Shang emperor to make all major decisions as well as day-to-day ones. In recent years, vaults have been discovered that contain thousands of tortoiseshells with inscriptions interpreting the cracks. These serve as a record of the history of the Shang peoples.

An outgrowth of the tortoiseshell oracles was the *I Ching*, a method using yarrow stalks, and later coins. It was brought to the West in the early twentieth century by Richard Wilhelm, who translated the Chinese text into German. Wilhelm believed the *I Ching* was one of the most significant books of world literature. The famed psychotherapist Carl Jung learned of the *I Ching* from Wilhelm, and saw it as the confirmation of his own theories that a level of reality exists beyond the notion of cause and effect.

China, of course, wasn't the only ancient culture to utilize oracles. Bones, shells, seeds, stones, sticks, animal skins and entrails, and other divinatory tools were used among traditional cultures in Africa, Europe, and the Americas. The Yoruba of Nigeria used cowrie shells; the Nankapi in northeastern Canada consulted bear and caribou bone oracles; and the Inca read the entrails of sacrificial llamas. The Norse of northern Europe threw Rune Stones, and Tarot cards were probably derived from the ancient Egyptian *Book of Thoth*. Even today, among surviving traditional cultures, divination is widely practiced. For example, the Kogi, an Indian culture in northern Colombia, toss colored stones into shallow pools of water to divine the future.

Fears about the power of divinatory tools and those who employed them led to taboos on their use. Until the fifteenth century, for instance, Tarot cards were alternately banned or approved by the Church and heads of state in Europe and England. Even today, some conservative religious factions frown on the cards. The most extreme examples of sanctions against oracles are found in the fundamentalist Moslem world, where even weather forecasts are forbidden.

Another perspective on oracles is found in the rationalist scientific viewpoint. Since oracles don't work according to the rules of cause and effect, they are regarded by most scientists as illogical and not worthy of serious consideration. This philosophy, known as reductionism, remains the current scientific paradigm, or worldview. From this perspective, no reality exists beyond cause-and-effect occurrences, and all consciousness can or will eventually be explained through biological mechanisms such as the brain's neurotransmitters. From the reductionist's viewpoint, oracles are considered to be vestiges of superstitious times, gimmicks used by gypsies and charlatans, or simply a passing fad.

Yet a new scientific paradigm is in the process of emerging, along with a renewed interest in oracular tools. A growing number of scientists—among them quantum physicists and Jungian analysts—see oracles as a significant clue in the search for a "multiverse"—a world in which reality has many meanings. Such pioneers are aware that oracles, rather than fragments of old superstitions, are focal points for releasing images from the unconscious mind. In essence, these scientists on the frontiers of research are building a bridge between the inner world and the outer world.

WHAT IS COLOR?

How, you may wonder, does color fit alongside the Runes, the Tarot, and the *I Ching*? Before exploring the mystical side of color, let's begin with a practical definition of terms.

Color, at the mundane level, is what we see when light rays reflect off objects. The particular hue depends upon the wavelength of the light striking the cells of color-sensitive cones in the retina at the back of the eye. When struck by photons—the primary particles of light waves—these cells fire, sending signals along the optic nerve to the brain. The longest visible wave is seen as the color red, while the shortest visible wave is violet. Although there are shorter and longer light waves, the eye does not perceive them as colors.

However, there is more to color than what meets the eye. Colors can be sensed as well as seen. We talk of "feeling blue," or "seeing red." We may know someone who is "green with envy," and we talk of "grey areas" and "blue Monday." We matter-of-factly think of colors in terms of the emotions or the sensations they produce in us. We speak of colors that are hot or icy, somber or gay, soothing or harsh.

The reason color affects us in such ways is related to what Carl Jung called "archetypes" of the unconscious mind. In other words, each color generates feelings or moods within us that are universal. Within the spectrum of colors visible to the human eye are representations of every possible emotional experience. Since colors represent the major archetypes of human experience, they can serve the same divinatory function as other oracles. Like the Tarot, the astrological zodiac, the *I Ching*, or the Runes, color speaks to us in symbols and unlocks the unconscious mind.

COLOR THROUGHOUT HISTORY

In ancient times, color was considered a vital force of the cosmos. In describing the influences of the planets, astrologers attributed colors to them. Mercury was associated with azure blue; Venus with turquoise and pink; Mars with red; Jupiter with green; Saturn with black; Uranus with mingled shades and changeable colors; and Neptune with the colors of the ocean. The Sun was associated with gold, and the Moon with silver.

Colors were also given numerical equivalents: black, one; yellow, two; purple, three; orange, four; blue, five; green, six; grey, seven; brown, eight; red, nine.

Number/Color Correspondences

1	Black	4	Orange	7	Grey
2	Yellow	5	Blue	8	Brown
3	Purple	6	Green	9	Red

Color holds sacred significance in many religious writings. In describing humans, the Hindu *Upanishads* state: "There are in his body the veins called *hita*, which are as small as a hair divided a thousandfold, full of white, blue, yellow, green, and red."

Other ancient Hindu texts describe seven "chakras" or "force-centers" of the body, each of which is associated with a color. These centers are invisibly connected to an equally nonmaterial etheric energy system surrounding the human body called the "aura." The colors of the chakra fall in a rainbowlike arrangement from the lower spine to the crown of the head. The lower spine is associated with red; the spleen with orange; the solar plexus with yellow; the heart with green; the throat with blue; the brow with indigo; and the crown with violet. In the yoga system, the colors differ somewhat from those in the Hindu religious texts. The heart is associated with yellow and the solar plexus with green. For more information on chakras, see page 264.

Spiritual masters throughout history have also been associated with colors. Buddha is correlated with yellow and gold. Of him it was written: "No sooner had he set his right foot within the city gate than the rays of six different colors which issued from his body rose hither and thither over palaces and pagodas, and decked them, as it were, with the yellow sheen of gold, or with the colors of a painting." Confucius, who was also identified with the color yellow, didn't care for the color purple. He wrote: "I hate the purple color, because it confuses us with the red color. I hate the goody-goodies because they confuse us with the virtuous people."

Judeo-Christian lore also includes numerous references to colors. Ezekiel (1:28) likened God to a rainbow: "As the appearance of the bow that is in the cloud in the day of rain, so was the appearance of the brightness round about. This was the appearance of the likeness of the glory of the Lord." Christ was associated with jasper and sardonyx—both reddish-brown. The Book of Revelations (5:3) states: "And He that sat was to look upon like a jasper and a sardine stone; and there was a rainbow round about the throne, in sight like unto an emerald."

The Jewish historian Flavius Josephus, writing in the first century A.D., ascribed white, purple, blue, and red colors to the four elements—earth, water, air, and fire. He wrote: "The veils, too, which were composed of four things, they declared the four elements; for the plain [white] linen was proper to signify the earth, because the flax grows out of the earth; the purple signified the sea, because the color is dyed by the blood of a sea shellfish; the blue is fit to signify the air; and the scarlet will naturally be an indication of fire."

The ancient Greeks also linked colors to the four elements. Aristotle wrote in *De Coloribus*: "Simple colors are the proper colors of the elements." Many of Aristotle's ideas on color were adapted from Plato, who wrote extensively on the nature of color. In *Phaedo*, he described the "true earth" as a place ascending into the ethers, where colors were extraordinary, and a "sight for the eyes of the blessed."

Navajo and Pueblo Indians not only associated colors with the elements, but also with the sexes. They considered red, yellow, and black to be masculine colors; white, blue, and green were feminine. Red also signified the day; black symbolized the night. To the Cherokee, red represented success, while blue indicated defeat. White stood for peace; and black for death.

In the Mayan cosmology, colors were linked with the four cardinal points. White represented North, the place of wisdom and purification; red was East, the place of light and generation; yellow was South, the place of life and expansion; and black was West, the place of death and transformation. The sky was held up at each corner or cardinal point by gods who were colored according to the direction they represented. North American Indian tribes, such as the Navajo, Hopi, Cherokee, Chippewa, and Creek also attributed colors to the four directions, but the colors varied from tribe to tribe.

The Egyptians created color halls in their temples, such as the ones at Karnak and Thebes, where the principles of color were studied. In their teachings, red was known as the color of the life force and corresponded with the body; yellow, the color of the intellect, was associated with the mind; and blue, signifying inspiration and tranquility, was linked with the spirit.

COLOR IN OUR CULTURE

Today, our unconscious response to the nature of color can be readily seen in popular culture. *White Nights* is a movie about two people of diverse backgrounds forced by circumstances to live together for a time, and who slowly come to understand each other. White is the color of understanding. *The Color Purple* is a book and a film about a young woman who lives in a highly restrictive environment. Purple speaks of restrictions and limitations.

In the film *The Color of Money*, each of the three characters grows as an individual by the end of the story. While green is indeed the color of money, it is also the color of growth. Two other films, *A Patch of Blue* and the *Blue Lagoon*, deal with isolation, sensitivity, and loneliness. Warren Beatty's film *Reds* is about human passions, political fervor, and emotional and environmental stress.

In the classic film *The Wizard of Oz*, Dorothy and her friends seek the wizard by following a yellow brick road. When they find him, the message of the wizard is: Don't rely on wizards—think for yourself. By using your own mind, you are transformed. Yellow signifies the intellect. The wizard resides in the Emerald City of Oz, a place where the houses, clothing, and even the people are green, because everyone wears green-tinted glasses. Dorothy and her friends come to terms with themselves in the Emerald City, and each one grows as a result. Green is not only the color of growth, it also signifies healing and rebirth.

Were the scriptwriters or producers of these movies consciously thinking about what the colors meant when they selected them for the name or theme? Maybe. But it's more likely that they didn't think about it at all. They probably just knew what color to use because it felt right. The fact is, you don't have to think about color for it to affect you. It just does.

In Hollywood's Universal City, the executive building of Universal Studios is referred to as the Black Tower. In New York, the CBS headquarters is called Black Rock. If you happen to mention either building by those names people usually react as if something ominous might be going on there. Black signifies things that are hidden or private. Both buildings are places where important decisions are made behind closed doors.

Even when color decisions are made intentionally, they sometimes produce psychological side effects. In its first two years "Miami Vice" was a big hit. It was a television series with a color code—bright tropical pastels and no earth tones. But by the end of the second season, the raves turned to digs about the quality of the scripts. One of the most noticeable ways the producers reacted was to shift the color scheme. Out went the vibrant pastels, and in came the darker, sullen tones. It was meant to bring new life to the series, but it also seemed as if the new colors themselves reflected the producers' defensive stance.

COLORS IN FASHION AND FUNCTION

The subtle influence of colors can also be seen in the color of clothes worn in certain types of professions. Nurses and doctors commonly wear white, the color of understanding and emotional reserve, attributes required for their stressful jobs. Surgeons and operating room nurses wear green, the color of healing.

Police are known as the Men in Blue, because of the common color of their uniforms. Since their job is to keep the peace, it's a natural choice. The color also has a soothing effect on the officers, whose job at any moment may entail violent confrontations. Tan or brown is also worn by some police departments and security forces. The color appropriately represents stability. They are, in fact, the community's stabilizers. Imagine how police and the public would react if law enforcement officers wore deep red, a hue of anger, hostility, and stress, the color hunters wear.

In American history, one police force did wear red, and fared poorly. They were British soldiers, known as Redcoats, at the time of the American Revolution. During America's civil war, the battle was between the North and the South, also known as the Yankees and Rebels or the Blue and Grey. Blue aptly represented the North's devotion or sensitivity to the union, while grey—the color of confusion—symbolized the fractured "dis-union" the South represented.

Traditional religious colors also reflect subtle unconscious meanings. During public appearances, the Pope wears white, a color representing understanding and detachment. Cardinals wear scarlet, a combination of red and blue, which evokes deep devotion and emotions. Purple is a color associated with the season of Lent, a period of fasting, penitence, and self-denial. Purple speaks of the color of established ways, rules, and limitations. Monks and Hasidic Jews wear black, aptly a color related to what is hidden.

In architecture and interior design, popular colors of periods reflected the feelings of the times. For example, the Twenties were a time of optimism and prosperity, and ushered in Art Deco, which featured pastels—blues, greens, pinks, and turquoise. In the Fifties, colonial style houses were popular. Their predominant browns and brick red represented security and stability, a theme of the times.

In fashion, colors popular during certain periods have also reflected the times. In the Forties, during World War II, tan, khaki, and olive drab, shades associated with peace, were

popular—a natural choice. These colors also denoted security. That was followed by black and white and solid colors as
the war ended. It was a time when everyone was looking for
order and clarity, and the colors reflected it. A short time
later, bright colors suddenly permeated fashion. The war was
over. Everything was imbued with brightness, matching the
outlook of the times. By the Fifties, beige and pastels were
popular, reflecting a time of peace and prosperity.

By the late Sixties, fashions were infused with a burst of
vibrant, psychedelic colors—reds, greens, purples. The colors symbolized the cultural upheaval taking place. Color itself became part of the new awareness. While bedazzling
wardrobes became everyday wear for some, a slogan—Black
is Beautiful—also took hold during the same period. Black
symbolizes what is hidden and feared, but combined with
"beautiful," it signified the emergence of what was hidden, in
this case a race and a culture.

By the late 1970s, the new awareness of color led to the
emergence of "color consultants," a response to the bestseller
Color Me Beautiful. Suddenly, women and men were having
their "colors done" and finding out if they were springs, win-
ters, falls, or summers—the categories author Carol Jackson
used to distinguish color types. That book was followed by
Color for Men, but men were already looking beyond the traditional male greys, blacks, blues, and browns and opening up
to soft pastels and even hot pinks. Colorful clothes had
broken the sex barrier. Color was seen as a way of expressing
oneself.

Changes were ahead, however. By the late 1980s, black
had become a virtual color code in fashion for men and wo-

men. One buyer for a department store, quoted in a newspaper article in early 1988, said that three-quarters of the women's dresses she ordered were black. Ironically, the interest in black clothing paralleled an economic development known as Black Friday—October 9, 1987—the day the stock market crashed. Black Friday and black clothing may well indicate an unconscious concern about the hidden future. In the aftermath of Black Friday, many people were concerned about whether or not life would continue along the path of economic growth and relative peace and prosperity.

Looking to the 1990s, the Color Association of the United States anticipates strong, bright colors—orange-reds, marigold yellow, bright greens and chartreuse—will be popular. The Color Association studies trends in art, fashion, architecture, and lighting to decide which colors will be used in interior design. Bright colors, however, aren't the only color factors on the horizon. The Association also sees a counter-trend emerging in color in the Nineties. Contrasting the bright colors will be a drift toward mauve grey—a grey with a cast of purple—as well as a range of blues and greens and pinks.

If those expectations come to pass, we may encounter a time of political and social upheaval. Lines will be clearly drawn. Conflicts will be intense and vivid, with sharp contrasts in points of view. Very little will be hidden or obscured. People will be forthright and open about their views. The confrontations, however, will cause considerable confusion. The pull of the past, when times were more tranquil, will be strong, resulting in a conservative backlash to the changes taking place.

THE STUDY OF COLOR

The resurgence of interest in color in the late Sixties also stimulated new research into color and the deep effects it has on us. Interestingly, some of the studies supported the notions of the ancients. Max Luscher, a German psychologist and author of *The Luscher Color Test*, created a method of character analysis using colored cards. Basing his own interpretations on studies of people's attitudes about colors, Luscher found that red represents energy; dark blue quiet and passivity; and bright yellow hope and activity. In the color halls of their temples, the Egyptians found similar meanings for red, yellow, and blue.

Other experiments cited by Luscher have shown that when people concentrate on the color red, they register increases in blood pressure, respiration, and heartbeat—traits of excitement. When blue is the color contemplated, the opposite occurs and they experience a calming effect—the blood pressure lowers, and the breathing and heartbeat slow.

A study reported in 1984 in the *International Journal of Biosocial Research* found that by changing the color and lighting schemes at a school in Wetaskiwin, Alberta, Canada, the IQ scores of some students jumped and absenteeism and disciplinary problems decreased. In the study, visual arts professor Harry Wohlfarth of the University of Alberta replaced orange, white, beige, and brown with yellow and blue, and exchanged fluorescent light bulbs for full-spectrum ones.

The widespread use of bubble-gum pink rooms to calm delinquents and criminals was the result of research by clinical psychologist Alexander Schauss, director of the American

Institute of Biosocial Research in Tacoma, Washington. In 1979, Schauss studied the response of subjects who stared at this pink hue on a piece of cardboard. He reported in the *Bulletin of the Psychonomic Society* that the color so relaxed the subjects that they did not perform simple strength tests as well as they did when viewing other hues. Today, pink rooms are commonplace in hundreds of institutions.

A 1987 study by Thomas Gilovich, a Cornell University professor of psychology, found that athletes who wear black are not only most likely to be viewed as the bad guys, but to act accordingly. Gilovich found that the most penalized football and hockey teams are those who wear black uniforms. In one experiment, forty students and twenty referees were shown videotapes of staged football plays, one with the tackler wearing a black uniform and one with the tackler wearing white. While the plays were nearly identical, viewers were more prone to call a penalty on the players in black.

As noted earlier, black signifies the unknown or hidden. Things unknown often incite feelings of fear and therefore take on negative connotations, whether this is warranted or not. And, as Gilovich found, people act accordingly.

Most of the early studies of color in this century were instigated by industry. Manufacturers wanted to know the effects of colors on their product, and to a lesser degree, on the workplace. Some of the findings of industrial studies have found that sugar doesn't sell well in green packages, nor do facial preparations in brown jars. Factory workers find light green boxes lighter and easier to lift than dark-colored ones. A factory with dark grey and blue walls found that absenteeism fell when the color scheme was lightened.

In a September 1987 newspaper article, Ford Motor Company's manager of Color Development Design advised against buying a green car. She warned that a company study found them to be difficult to sell. Although the study didn't distinguish light greens from darker greens, it's interesting that the darker or intensified green denotes deceit, treachery, and duplicity. Who'd want to buy a car whose color was beaming out that sort of message?

DIVINING YOUR OWN COLOR SENSE

The fact that there is a common thread in the meaning of colors—that ancient Egyptians and twentieth-century scientists hit upon the same meanings, that color trends in fashion and architecture reflect societal trends—leaves little doubt that colors are indeed an undeniable part of our collective unconscious. You can find your own proof through your experiments with the color cubes of the *Rainbow Oracle*.

The *Rainbow Oracle* is a modern divinatory device that draws upon the storehouse of knowledge in our unconscious minds. Like the images on Tarot cards or the Rune Stones, they reflect archetypal meanings. Yet, there is a subtle difference. Color is immediate, familiar, and everywhere. It constantly affects us.

When the *Rainbow Oracle* was asked what it thought of itself, the colors orange, yellow, red, and green were thrown. Using the four-color method described later, here is what the oracle said about itself:

The first color, orange, falls in the position of *Surrounding Influences*, which undoubtedly refers to the authors and editor. Orange speaks of balance, and infers that the authors and editor are seeking to balance the practical with the esoteric.

The second color thrown was yellow. It appears in the *Obstacle* position. The indication is that the obstacle faced is the task of keeping everything in order. Yellow is the color of logic, and when dealing with an oracle based on the intuitive, there is a tendency to overlook logic and order.

The oracle's *Past* is reflected in the color red. In the spiritual context, red triggers the powerhouse of the unconscious mind. That, in essence, is what the oracle is about—the triggering of the unconscious.

The fourth roll relates to the *Outcome*. The color was green, the hue of healing, rebirth, and growth. This suggests that the oracle will serve to expand the awareness of those who use it. In a spiritual context, green refers to a renewal of interest in matters of higher consciousness.

In the chapters ahead, you will be shown how to use the colors of the rainbow to activate your unconscious mind. To prepare yourself for the adventure, we suggest that you begin by reading the guidelines in the following chapter.

2
HOW BEST TO USE
THE ORACLE

B EFORE INTRODUCING
the specifics of the various types of Rainbow Readings, it's important that you understand a few guidelines about the use of the *Rainbow Oracle* as a divinatory tool. Some of the guidelines will be explained in greater depth later on in the text.

PREPARE YOURSELF. An oracle is only as clear as you are. Therefore, the first thing you need to do before you begin posing questions to the oracle is to relax and clear your mind. Just take a few moments to close your eyes, to calm yourself, and to shift your focus from your outer world to your inner one. If you are nervous or emotionally upset, your passport to the inner world is invalid. Wait to consult the oracle until the storm has passed.

KEEP A NOTEBOOK. Write down your questions, and the colors of the Rainbow Readings you throw, listing each color in its appropriate position. You might add a word or two from the color keys, or actually transcribe important insights found in the readings. Later, you'll be able to verify the accuracy of the color commentaries you've cast. Your notebook can serve as a "Rainbow Journal" of your life.

BEGIN WITH THE ONE-CUBE READING. This simple method is a good introduction to the oracle, and will allow you to see how it works at the most basic level. The questions are already provided (see p. 33), and there are no distinctions made between the intensified (slashed) colors and the normal colors for this method.

PHRASE YOUR QUESTIONS CAREFULLY. When preparing questions for the more complex four- and six-cube Rainbow Readings, keep in mind that the oracle reacts to the precise way you state your concern. Even the slightest change in wording can make a considerable difference. Be specific. If your question is vague, expect a vague answer.

Avoid asking "yes" or "no" questions, or ones calling for a specific date. For example, don't ask, "Will I get a raise next month?" or "When will I get a raise?" Ask instead, "What is the outlook for receiving a raise within the next month?" You'll find the word "outlook" is a handy one that works well in a variety of circumstances.

HOW TO THROW THE CUBES. First of all, remember to focus on your question during the entire process of rolling the color cubes. For each position in the readings, roll the cubes around in your hand for a moment and—without looking—choose one, or allow one to fall from your hand. Take the selected cube, shake it in your hand for another moment, then roll it out, just as though you were playing at dice. The color that lands face up is the color for that position. Write down the position and the color rolled. Then—and this is very important—return all FIVE cubes to your hand for each position to be rolled, and repeat the selection process described above. (If two cubes happen to fall out of your hand instead of just one, that's an additional message from the oracle. Read both colors for the selected position in the Rainbow Reading.)

KNOW THE TERMS. There are several key terms that are repeatedly used in the *Rainbow Oracle*. Knowing their meanings will help make the oracle easy to use. These terms are:

COLOR KEYS: These are the summary meanings of the colors given at the beginning of each color listed in Chapter 7, Interpretations.

INTENSIFIED COLORS: These are easily identified by the diagonal white slashes across the darker shades of red, orange, yellow, green, blue, purple, pink, and brown. These intensified (slashed) colors indicate an intensification of the meaning or energy associated with a color. For example, a normal cube roll of red indicates high energy. However, a cube roll of intensified red—listed as Red (I)—means great stress. A roll of yellow refers to intellect and logic, but intensified yellow—Yellow (I)—stands for being overly logical and rigid. Rolling an intensified color *does not mean you're getting a negative reading.* But it may serve as a warning to look carefully at the issues, while also suggesting how you might initiate the changes needed to improve the situation.

POSITION: This term indicates the placement of a color in a four- or six-color Rainbow Reading.

Positions in a Four-Color Reading

1. Surrounding influences
2. Obstacles faced
3. Past
4. Outcome

Positions in a Six-Color Reading
1. Surrounding influence
2. Obstacles faced
3. Past
4. Present
5. Future (1–3 months)
6. Future (4–6 months)

The meanings of these positions are:

Surrounding Influences—This is the first position in the four- or six-color Rainbow Reading. It refers to any indirect or environmental factors influencing the matter of concern—in essence, the ambience surrounding the question. For example, if you ask about job advancement, the Surrounding Influences would include any effects created by fellow workers, by the work setting, by your number of years on the job, your current salary, etc.

Obstacles faced—This represents the second position in a four- or six-color reading. It refers to the factor or factors that are blocking the resolution of a concern.

Past—The third position in a four- or six-color reading relates to past events affecting the matter in question.

Present—This is the fourth position in a six-color reading. It refers to what is happening at present concerning your question.

Outcome—This is the fourth and last position in a four-color reading. It refers to whatever is coming to pass related to your question. If you don't like the answer, consider the Obstacle and what you can do to change it. All of us have the power to transform the end result of any situation.

Future—This represents the fifth *and* the sixth positions in a six-color reading. The Future in the fifth position relates to upcoming events in the next one to three months. The Future in the sixth position relates to upcoming events in the next four to six months.

ANSWER CATEGORY: This term refers to the three possible levels of interpretation for each color position in *both* the four- and six-color Rainbow Readings. Each question addressed to the oracle will relate to one of the following three categories:

Emotional—This category relates to interpretations for all questions in the Rainbow Readings that deal with relationships, partnerships, inner sentiments, and psychological issues.

Material—The second category of interpretation relates to questions about business, finances, careers, money, and all material concerns.

Spiritual—The third category relates to concerns about one's spiritual path, quest, or vision.

KNOW THE CATEGORY OF YOUR QUESTION. When interpreting a four- or six-color reading, make sure you know which category your concern really fits—Emotional, Material, or Spiritual. Focus on that section of the interpretation. Occasionally, it is possible that deeper questions might cover more than one category. Perhaps a marriage might be going through financial difficulties. In such a case, you would read the interpretations for both the Emotional and the Material categories.

DON'T BECOME DEPENDENT ON THE ORACLE. The information you obtain from any oracle should simply be an adjunct to what you already know, a second opinion. It's like seeking counsel from a close friend whose opinion you trust. Hopefully, you don't ask that friend for guidance at every fork in the road. If you did, your friend would not be a friend, but a controller. The same is true of an oracle. Don't turn the oracle into a mindless method of being told what to do with your life. Consult it wisely, and always think for yourself.

THERE ARE NO NEGATIVE READINGS. When you roll one of the "intensified" colors—those designated by a diagonal white slash—there is no reason to panic or to think that you're getting a negative answer. You may not always like what you're being told, but the oracle would be ineffective and inaccurate if the responses were always cheery aphorisms or innocuous platitudes. The fact is, the path to the light is often shrouded in darkness. Whenever you receive an answer that seems negative, look at it as a learning experience.

If all of the cubes you roll in a reading are intensified colors, take the reading seriously. Think carefully about each of the cubes' responses. You're probably not seeing things clearly in your life. You're taking everything to the extreme, and need more balance. However, if you take steps to deal with the situation, you may be moved onto a profound new path.

PUT YOUR FREE WILL TO USE. Some people are afraid to use an oracle because they think they won't like what they find out, and that then they'll be committed to whatever it says. Remember, nothing is unchangeable. At an unconscious level, you know where you're heading. The oracle simply draws upon that knowledge. If you don't like the direction— change it! The outcome is always up to you.

IT'S THE MESSAGE, NOT THE MESSENGER. The color cubes are simply a means of triggering the contents of the unconscious mind. They have no power of their own, and there is no reason to treat them with any more reverence than you would any other inanimate object. Of course, you don't want to lose them, so keep the cubes in the bag made for their storage.

DON'T ASK THE SAME QUESTION REPEATEDLY. Whenever you use any divinatory tool, the first answer is the accurate one. Requestioning the oracle will result in responses pertaining to varying aspects of the question, and will probably cause more confusion than clarity.

EXPAND THE MEANING AND METHODS. Over time, the subtle and more individualized nuances of the meanings of each color will become more apparent. With practice and mastery, you may add your own personal interpretations to the meanings, and develop your own methods. When a particular color repeatedly appears for a certain type of question, study the meaning closely. How does it apply specifically to you? For example, if you were involved in agriculture, green in a career question might signify the growth of crops rather than professional growth and advancement in another type of career. Likewise, once you've mastered the basics of the systems described in the following chapters, you might experiment with other methods, perhaps a five-cube system in which you toss all the cubes at once. While the methods we've presented have been thoroughly researched, you may find others to be equally valid.

BE SENSITIVE TO OTHERS. When you roll the color cubes with friends, be aware that you are opening doors that might otherwise remain locked between you and the other people. It's an effective way of opening communication. However, don't abuse it. Avoid using the *Rainbow Oracle* as a way of manipulating others.

THE *RAINBOW ORACLE* IS A TOOL, NOT A TASK. While the oracle should be taken seriously, it should always be a source of both learning and enjoyment. You are, in essence, an armchair explorer delving into the inner mysteries of life. Enjoy the adventure.

3
THE TOSS
OF THE CUBE

LET'S SAY YOU'VE NEVER tried any other method of divination, such as Tarot cards or *I Ching* coins. Now you've been presented with the idea that you can obtain answers to questions or gain insight into your life by rolling colored cubes. Your initial response is probably doubt. How could the roll of a color cube be anything but random chance?

The throw of the cubes is indeed a random process. However, when you are posing a question to the oracle, there is an inherent underlying pattern to that randomness. It's called synchronicity. That means that what appears to be random is actually a meaningful coincidence that relates to your question at that particular point in time and space.

The very nature of oracles defies the idea that we live in a universe that was created just by chance when the right combination of gases mixed and condensed to form matter, a planet, an atmosphere, and life. Oracles are testimony to the principle that a conscious creative force underlies all matter, and all supposedly chance events.

Oracles also demonstrate the power of belief. If you're convinced that the oracle cannot answer your questions, you will most likely find that to be true. However, if you leave an opening for yourself by considering that anything is possible, then you'll probably find accurate and possibly quite astonishing answers when you roll the color cubes.

With practice, you will gain confidence and find your abilities improving. What you're doing is attuning and developing your natural psychic abilities, opening the gates to an inner pool of knowledge. The oracle, in a sense, is an entry-level method of developing psychic talents, which are accessible to all who are willing to experiment and to keep an open mind.

MEET THE COLOR CUBES

To start out, take the cubes in your hands and get used to the feel of them. Examine the colors closely. Find the cube that has no "intensified" (slashed) colors. The colors on this cube are red, orange, yellow, green, blue, and purple. In addition to these six colors, the other cubes also contain pink, brown, peach, violet, gold, silver, grey, white, black, and a rainbow face—all of which appear once.

Eight of the colors appear another time in deeper or intensified shades that are easily identified by diagonal white slashes. These intensified colors include: red, orange, yellow, green, blue, purple, pink, and brown. The intensified colors carry different meanings than the lighter hues in the four- and six-cube Rainbow Readings. Please note that the one-cube readings are the only exception. In the one-cube readings, there is only one meaning for both shades.

There are NO intensified shades of peach, violet, gold, silver, grey, white, black, or the rainbow. In any of the subsequent listings of color interpretations, these colors will always follow after the colors that have intensifications (slashes).

The five separate cubes of the *Rainbow Oracle* are colored in the following manner:

COLOR CUBE FACETS

CUBE #1	CUBE #2	CUBE #3	CUBE #4	CUBE #5
Red	Red	Black	Silver	Blue
Orange	Yellow	White	Gold	Green
Yellow	Red (I)	Brown	Peach	Blue (I)
Green	Yellow (I)	Violet	Grey	Green (I)
Blue	Purple (I)	Rainbow	Pink	Orange (I)
Purple	Purple	Brown (I)	Pink (I)	Orange

Make sure you can identify the colors. Compare the peach with the pink, the purple with the violet, the silver with the grey, the intensified yellow with the intensified orange. Check the color spreads on each cube as listed above to make sure you know them. If you're still not certain, you might look over the cubes with a friend. The first six colors—red, orange, yellow, green, blue, and purple—are repeated twice on the cubes. The reason is that these are the colors most frequently mentioned when people are asked to quickly list a series of colors.

In the interpretation sections, you will find the colors listed in the following sequence: red, red (I), orange, orange (I), yellow, yellow (I), green, green (I), blue, blue (I), purple,

purple (I), pink, pink (I), brown, brown (I), peach, violet, gold, silver, grey, white, black, rainbow. This order begins with the eight colors that include a deeper or intensified shade.

PREPARING YOURSELF FOR A RAINBOW READING

Make sure you know why you're consulting the oracle. It's important to understand that an oracle is only as serious as you are. If your intent is to make a joke or a game out of it, don't expect relevant answers. If, however, you take the oracle for what it is, as a means of friendly guidance, you can expect helpful responses that reach the heart of the matter.

Before you throw the cubes, it's a good idea to relax and clear your mind for a moment. Close your eyes, take two or three deep breaths, and turn your focus inward. Let go of all other thoughts and concerns. If you are asking a specific question, focus your attention on this question before you throw. If you are using the twelve-color horoscope method and not asking a specific question, then concentrate on the idea that you will receive helpful guidance.

HOW TO THROW THE CUBES. First of all, take a few deep breaths and center yourself. Focus on your question, or your wish for guidance, and continue to do so during the entire process of rolling the color cubes. For each position in the readings, roll the color cubes around in your hand for a moment and—without looking—choose one, or allow one to fall from your hand. Take the selected cube and shake it in your hand for a moment and then roll it out, just as though you were playing at dice. The color that lands uppermost is the color for that position. Write down the position and the colors rolled. Then—and this is very important—return *all five cubes* to your hand for each position to be rolled, and repeat the selection process.

If two cubes happen to fall out of your hand instead of just one, that's an additional message from the oracle. Read both the colors that turn up in that fashion for the selected position in the Rainbow Reading.

KEEPING THE RECORD STRAIGHT

It's a good idea to keep a record of your readings in your "Rainbow Journal" because oftentimes the mind will distort matters, even within minutes of the reading. If you don't write down your questions, you probably won't remember the exact wording, and sometimes the omission or addition of one word will subtly change the meaning.

A "Rainbow Journal" also gives you a chance to look back and chart your personal progress and changes. The journal becomes a personal history, showing where you were then and where you are now. Date your entries, and leave room for key words or relevant passages from the interpretations to remind you of the meanings of your readings. In addition, the journal gives you a chance to check the accuracy of your readings later on.

HOW ACCURATE ARE THE READINGS?

If you took your blood pressure immediately after a heated argument, you might expect to find a higher than normal reading. It would appear that you have high blood pressure, even though you don't. Such a reading would not be an accurate picture of your health. Similarly, when you're consulting the oracle, if you are agitated or depressed or feeling particularly frenzied or angered, your Rainbow Readings may be equally misleading. If this is the way you're feeling, then you may be in the wrong state of mind for rolling the cubes. You'd be better off returning them to their pouch for the time being.

Even when your temperament is normal, you can expect occasional "mis-readings," especially if you ask the same question over and over again. If you consistently receive inaccurate readings, examine your thoughts. Why are you using the oracle? If the answer is to prove that it doesn't work, then you've done just that. Now, consider why it works for other people.

Like any divinatory tool, the *Rainbow Oracle* offers a perspective for a particular moment. Circumstances are fluid, and what may have applied for a specific matter last week may not be true today. The oracle provides patterns, and suggests tendencies, but it does not present an unalterable or fixed future. While you can gain insight and depth of perspective on particular matters, don't turn any divinatory tool into a slavish method of being told what to do with your life. Don't use it as a crutch that prevents you from taking action when action is required simply because you haven't had time to consult the oracle.

Use the guidance of the *Rainbow Oracle* as you would the advice of a close friend. Consider the responses you receive carefully. But keep in mind that it's up to you to make your own decisions. No one can live your life but you.

4
ONE-CUBE RAINBOW
READING

AN ORACLE DOESN'T
have to be a complicated process that requires lengthy study
before you can put it to use. The quickest and simplest form
of Rainbow Reading requires the toss of just one cube. Select
one of the fifteen questions you'll find listed on page 33;
shake all the cubes in your hand; select one, roll that cube,
and look up the answer according to the number of the question and the color rolled.

These "instant" answers, typically one to four sentences,
are simplified responses that don't include either the cause or
the effect of the concern. It's like finding out the temperature,
but not the full weather forecast. You hear that it's seventy-
two degrees now, but you don't know what the high or low
temperatures will be, or whether it's going to rain later. The
multi-cube methods, which are explained in later chapters,
offer more detailed responses. Still, the one-cube method can
be helpful and surprisingly precise.

The fifteen questions provided cover a wide range of
concerns that are most commonly asked during readings.
This is the only method of Rainbow Reading in which the
questions have been provided for you. Here they are:

QUESTIONS FOR THE ONE-CUBE ROLL

1) In what type of career will I find success?

2) How compatible am I with friends (family members)?

3) How do I fit in with the career I've chosen?

4) What is the outlook for my relationship with...?

5) What is my financial forecast?

6) Are there any upcoming changes in my career?

7) What changes are needed in my personal life?

8) What will be the outcome of my present venture?

9) What is the outlook of my proposed venture?

10) How will...react to my idea?

11) What energy should I put forth into my present thoughts?

12) What are my prospects for a new relationship?

13) What type of person should I look for?

14) What does...think of me?

15) Is "yes" the answer to my question? (Any question that is not listed above.)

You can ask a question for yourself or for others. For example, if you are concerned about a relationship, ask Question 4 and simply add the name of the person you're thinking about. On the other hand, if you want to ask about the relationship of two friends, Sarah and Mike, you would state the question in this manner: "What is the outlook for Sarah's relationship with Mike?" If you want to ask about Sarah's career, adjust Question 3 to read: "How does Sarah fit into the career she's chosen?"

You can also make questions more specific to your particular needs. For instance, if you want to know what you should do in order to advance your career, Question 11 would apply by adding to the end of it " . . . in order to advance at my career?" Say you've received a promotion and are now supervising the same people you used to work with. You want to know how you'll get along with them. In this case, you would adjust Question 2 to read: "How compatible am I with the people I'll be supervising?"

If you've been offered a new job, but are uncertain how you'll fare financially if you take it, add this phrase to Question 5: "What is my financial outlook if I take the new job?"

Question 9 can be adjusted to fit numerous situations. For example, say you're a musician playing with a band that performs regularly. The problem is that you're not getting an opportunity to sing, which is one of your strong talents. You're considering quitting and starting your own band. You would adjust Question 9 to read: "What is the outlook for my proposed venture—starting my own group?" You'd use the same question if you were concerned about an upcoming trip to Mexico. Adjust the question to read: "What's the outlook for my trip to Mexico?"

While you can adjust the wording to many of the questions to fit your circumstances, you should avoid changing the essence of the question. For example, Question 13 deals with people, not inanimate objects or conditions. So you can't change it to read: "What type of job should I look for?" For that, adjust Question 5. On the other hand, Question 5 deals with finances, so don't change it to ask a question about a relationship—use Question 4.

If you can't find any other way to express your concern, turn it into a "yes" or "no" question, and ask Question 15.

When you use the one-cube method of Rainbow Readings, you don't have to concern yourself with the intensified colors—the darker shades of the colors designated by a diagonal white slash. For the one-cube method only, it makes no difference whether the color rolled appears in its regular or intensified shade—the meaning will be the same. For example, if you roll brown or intensified brown, simply consult brown.

Now, look up the response to your question according to the color you roll. Each color is presented separately in the section on One-Cube Color Interpretations, and the responses to each of the fifteen questions are listed in numerical order under each color.

ONE-CUBE COLOR INTERPRETATIONS

RED

1) You would find success in any high-energy career that demands the most from you—a career with deadlines and risk. The key is that it must excite you. This could include a career as a broadcast journalist, as a stockbroker or commodity trader on Wall Street, an air traffic controller, a police officer, a surgeon, an emergency room worker, an ambulance driver. In other words, any type of career in which you are continually pushed to your limits.

2) You have strong emotional ties or intense relations with them, which sometimes causes stress.

3) Your career creates stressful situations, so you need to be highly motivated to cope. You may be putting so much energy into your career that you are a workaholic.

4) This combination makes for an emotionally intense relationship.

5) Your finances are not stable. You must put forth high energy to maintain a balanced financial status. Avoid negativity in your thoughts.

6) If you veer from a positive outlook, there may be problems in your career.

7) Slow down. Your personal life will be more stable if you are less intense.

8) There is stress and turmoil related to your present venture. Changes are needed in your thoughts to achieve success.

9) Your proposed venture needs to be examined more closely to avoid stress.

10) Expect a quick "yes" or "no" to your idea. Be careful when you approach this person with any volatile questions.

11) You need to add more energetic action to your present thinking. Don't procrastinate.

12) The prospects of a new, intense relationship are real, but it may not endure.

13) Seek a high-energy person, someone who is physically attractive to you.

14) That you are an excitable, passionate, sometimes hot-tempered person. This person will tend to be cautious around you.

15) At the moment there is too much stress surrounding the question for a "yes" or "no" answer. More thought on the subject is needed.

ORANGE

1) You would find success in any career requiring a balance of emotions and logic, and allowing a strong degree of pride in your work. Creative fields such as writing, advertising, commercial art, or publicity are a few possibilities.

2) You've reached a balance between mind and heart with those surrounding you.

3) Your career satisfies both your mind and emotions.

4) You've attained a level of understanding that is both emotional and practical.

5) Your finances stay constant. If you are in debt, financial balance will be achieved.

6) If your career is stable, its status will not change. If there is a lack of stability, then stability will be achieved.

7) If you carefully weigh your logic and emotions, you will see your personal life more clearly.

8) You'll be satisfied with the results of your present venture.

9) Success is likely in your proposed venture.

10) Everything you say will be carefully weighed and measured by the individual.

11) Stop trying to please those around you. Look within for the balance you seek.

12) A relationship that already exists may develop into something more.

13) Look for a warm, stable person who's capable of sharing his or her feelings.

14) You are regarded as a balanced person.

15) Yes, and it'll make you happy.

YELLOW

1) You would have success in any type of career that uses the intellect and logic, especially those dealing with contracts, written documents, or other legal matters. Some examples might be as a: lawyer, judge, professor, investigator, police officer, technical writer, computer programmer, casting or literary agent, stenographer or secretary.

2) Regarding friends, family, fellow workers, your logic rather than emotions are emphasized. You put those relationships all in their proper order.

3) The career you've chosen was a logical choice.

4) Look for an intellectual relationship. You've made the choice based on logic, rather than emotion.

5) You will make money through contracts, legal documents, financial speculation.

6) Look for a promotion. Your career status will change, and the adjustment most likely will be for the better.

7) Your approach to your personal life requires more logic, and less emotion.

8) Your present venture is in its proper order. There will be legal documentation of your efforts.

9) In order for your proposed venture to succeed, you must pay more attention to details.

10) Your ideas will be evaluated on the basis of logic, not emotion. You could receive a contract, or other legal documents.

11) To reach your objectives, place more emphasis on your present circumstances. Avoid being self-centered.

12) Stop looking for the perfect partner. Your rigid criteria are what's holding you back from finding the right person.

13) Look for someone with intelligence and refinement. You may spend more time talking than romancing.

14) You are seen as logical and intelligent.

15) Logically speaking, the answer is "yes."

GREEN

1) Any career involving new and innovative ideas is right for you. For example, you would have success placing a new product on the market, or involvement in businesses that are new ventures, or growing businesses. Other careers that might attract you include: the health professions, landscaping, research and development, investment banking, as well as any type of entrepreneurship.

2) Relationships grow on you. The longer you know a person, the more you trust him or her. You find new friends exciting.

3) You're now open to the growth and expansion of your career.

4) If you put time and energy into your relationship, it will grow.

5) Your finances are always changing. A small increase, such as a raise in pay or a bonus, is coming.

6) You grow as career opportunities present themselves. If there is no room for growth within the company, you will make changes.

7) Discard old, useless ideas. You must be open to change in your personal life.

8) You can expect changes in your present venture if you continue in the direction you're headed.

9) Creative changes must be made to ensure the growth and success of your proposed venture.

10) There will be a positive reaction to your ideas. You have planted the seeds. Now make them grow.

11) Revitalize your thinking. Discard the old and bring in the new.

12) A new relationship will be blossoming.

13) Look for someone who is full of life, an adaptable person with a ready smile.

14) Your flexibility and potential for growth are understood.

15) Yes—but don't be surprised if the answer changes quickly. The situation needs to progress further.

BLUE

1) The career for you is the one that allows you to make your own rules or to be your own boss. You're a private person, and may prefer working at home. Nonstressful jobs, and those allowing you to carry out tasks in your own way, are best for you. Some career categories include: independent craftsperson, such as a carpenter or plumber; the creative arts, such as fiction writer, painter, sculptor, or mime; fine arts worker, such as a jeweler; or perhaps as an independent consultant or psychotherapist, someone who works one-on-one.

2) You're basically a loner with private ideas and thoughts. You're capable of deep emotional ties. Yet you may not bring forth that feeling to others.

3) You need to feel more secure with your career. You must learn to speak out more to achieve success.

4) You have to learn to share your feelings and become less emotionally inhibited.

5) You will find more financial success if you put forth more aggressive energy toward your goals.

6) There are no career changes ahead. Your present status is maintained.

7) You need to go within yourself to become more aware of your feelings and thoughts.

8) Your present venture will bring peace of mind.

9) Your proposed venture has not been adequately clarified.

10) The response to your idea will be a quiet, inner reaction that may take time to surface.

11) You need to become more introspective in your present thinking. Set your own pace.

12) Don't enter into a new relationship out of desperation. Be cautious and discerning.

13) Seek a quiet, sensitive, and private person, one who enjoys the pleasures of home.

14) You are a sensitive, private person.

15) The answer to your question is "no." However, there is a possibility that this will change.

PURPLE

1) You're best suited for a career dealing with the past, or a job based on philosophical ideas. Possibilities might be: librarian, record-keeper, statistician, antique dealer, archaeologist, historian, minister or related religious fields. You might also find success in a job with lots of rules and regulations to guide you.

2) You compartmentalize your relationships into traditional roles. As a result, you may have a tendency to restrict or repress yourself or others.

3) If you understand the restrictions and limitations and follow an established path, you will move ahead.

4) Any new relationship will be based on past emotions. It's as if you were on a merry-go-round. You choose different colored horses, but still cling to the same rings. Because of self-imposed restrictions or repressed feelings, you may hit a stalemate with a partner.

5) There are financial restrictions and limitations ahead.

6) There are only limited changes ahead. You will face many restrictions.

7) You need to organize your personal life. Set goals, and don't be too easy with yourself.

8) You can only go so far with your present venture. There are inherent limitations.

9) Be alert to restrictions and limitations in your proposed venture. It can only go so far.

10) Your idea will be regarded cautiously. It will face many restrictions.

11) Look to the lessons from the past to better focus your thinking for the future.

12) More of the same. Be careful you don't repeat patterns of the past.

13) Look to the past to see what qualities you enjoyed in other meaningful relationships, and use that as a guide.

14) You might be seen as inhibited or someone who dwells in the past.

15) The answer to your question is "yes," but there will be limitations.

PINK

1) Since pink is the color of vitality and health and sensitivity, you may be drawn to the health-related professions or those that allow you to express your inner sensitivity. They may range on the one hand from nurse or sex therapist to a health food entrepreneur or a physical education instructor. On the other hand, you may be drawn to the beauty or fashion industry or to the cosmetics field and professions such as make-up artist, fashion model, hair stylist, or even plastic surgeon.

2) You are very compatible with family and friends because you are sensitive to their needs and concerns. You are very well liked.

3) The vitality and aura of happiness that surround you make you adaptable to varying situations in your career.

4) There is a great deal of love and romance between you and your partner. The aspects are favorable.

5) Success is inevitable. There is no need for concern.

6) There are no major changes ahead, but growth is possible if you revitalize your thinking.

7) You need to add a little more romance to your personal life.

8) Because of your vitality and enthusiasm, success in your present venture is ensured.

9) The success of your proposed venture may depend upon your own health and energy.

10) The response to your idea may not be as strong as you would like. You may feel as though you are being placated, but keep a positive view.

11) Turn your thoughts to love and renewed vitality. Visualize your body as sound and healthy.

12) Focus on love and romance. Leave yourself open to commitment.

13) Look for a loving person, a classic romantic.

14) You are seen as someone who has a great deal of vitality and love to give. People are attracted to you.

15) The answer to your question is "yes." You will be pleased with the outcome of your inquiry.

BROWN

1) Since brown is related to the Earth and to stability, you would fare well in established, tried and true careers. Possibilities include dealing with the land, such as a career in real estate or agriculture. Other possibilities are careers dealing with money, such as a banker or accountant, but not ones where your livelihood is based on a high degree of risk or financial speculation. You may also be drawn toward secure government jobs, such as a career diplomat or postal worker; or jobs related to home and stability such as homemaker, daycare or preschool worker, tutor, or nanny. This could also include a career in social work dealing with people's concerns about stability.

2) Relationships are extremely important to you. They are based on your need for emotional security.

3) You have established a firm career base that leads to material security.

4) The relationship has a firm foundation. The seeds you've planted will grow.

5) Material and financial success are indicated.

6) No changes are needed. Your career has a firm base that is an incentive for growth.

7) Establish a more secure base for your personal life. Then growth can be guaranteed.

8) Your present venture will establish a firm base with material gain.

9) Bring your proposed venture back to the basics and let it grow from the ground up.

10) A reaction to your idea will be positive and probably lead to material gain. It has a strong foundation.

11) Get your thinking back down to Earth. Focus your thoughts on a firmer foundation.

12) A person with a stabilizing influence on you will be entering your life.

13) Seek someone who can provide both material and emotional security.

14) You are seen as a stable person who is practical and down to Earth.

15) The answer to your question is a definite "yes."

PEACH

1) You have the versatility to deal with both the logical and the emotional side of people and situations in a profession. Possible careers might be: counselor, arbitrator, liaison person, ambassador, or publicist. (Also see responses for this question under pink and yellow.)

2) You're too mellow. Take care that your easygoing nature doesn't make you a doormat.

3) You are the key ingredient in the success of your career. You create your own reality.

4) You are the master of your emotions. You can create dissension or love, whichever you choose.

5) Your financial prospects are brighter than you think.

6) The only changes ahead in your career are those you choose.

7) You need to mellow out. Don't be too emotional or logical. Seek a middle ground.

8) Since you are in control of your present venture, the answer is up to you.

9) The success of your proposed venture will depend on your measuring and weighing of the circumstances.

10) You can expect a balanced response to your idea only if you keep a positive perspective.

11) Balance your feelings. Determine whether or not your present thoughts are contributing to what you want.

12) A mellow affair may be in the offing. Don't try to force things; let them happen.

13) Don't settle for just anyone. Look for someone who balances your needs.

14) You are regarded as an appealing, likeable sort of individual who has his or her life in order.

15) The answer to the question is "yes," providing there is a balance.

VIOLET

1) You are well suited for any type of work where high-minded thinking is involved. Examples would be careers related to mastery, or the highest ideals of any profession, especially ones involving humanitarian, spiritual, or transcendent thought. Teachers of philosophy or religion would fit here, as would any higher order of work, ranging from a chess player who is a life master, to a corporate executive involved in international humanitarian work, to a statesman in the highest sense of the profession.

2) You expect the highest ideals to imbue relationships with friends and family. You want them to be on their best behavior.

3) You're attuned to your career. You look for the higher purpose of your work.

4) You're forging a spiritual bond. You may be transcending the physical aspects. It could be a Platonic relationship.

5) By keeping a positive financial outlook and not allowing feelings of greed to enter, you should do well.

6) By focusing on the highest, most positive aspects of your career, you could improve your situation.

7) You should seek the higher mind or spiritual aspects in your personal life. Express universal love for all.

8) The results of your present venture will be positive. They lead to a higher order of understanding.

9) If the proposed venture is of a positive nature and not being undertaken merely for material gain, you could profit from it.

10) The response to your thinking may surprise you. The focus will be on the higher order of your idea.

11) Concentrate on the higher order of thought. Learn to commune with your spiritual self. Avoid any selfish motives.

12) A Platonic relationship will develop. You will seem extremely attuned to the other person.

13) Seek a spiritually minded person, someone you can feel free to talk with about the things that really matter to you.

14) You are regarded as a caring and aware person.

15) The answer to your question is "yes," but only if the good of all is concerned.

GOLD

1) With your energy and ambitions, you should be successful at almost any type of profession you choose. You will make it happen.

2) You are a positive person, and you work at all your relationships. You are likely to achieve the goals you seek with them.

3) You are goal oriented and successful. Once a goal has been attained, you continue to reach higher and higher.

4) There is a magnetic attraction between you and your friend.

5) You have the Midas touch, and achieve success and abundance. The goals you set will be attained.

6) Changes are ahead, and they are all for the best.

7) You need to set specific personal goals. A life with no direction goes nowhere.

8) As long as you've firmly established your goals, success is promised in your present venture.

9) Your proposed venture will be realized. Look for the pot of gold at the end of the rainbow.

10) The idea has all the makings of a winner. You will prosper by it.

11) Be aware of your potential for achievement. Think positive. Know you are a winner. There is no room for negative thoughts.

12) A meaningful relationship is possible. Be prepared to make a commitment.

13) Seek out an ambitious and supportive person who will appreciate and applaud your success.

14) You are recognized as a high achiever, a successful, goal-oriented individual.

15) The answer to your question is "yes," and the results will be beyond your wildest dreams.

SILVER

1) Look for a career that requires imagination, intuition, risk taking, or vision. Possible careers include: financial consultant, speculator, psychic, futurist, architect, science fiction writer, planner, and creator of all sorts. You are the sort of person who is often the visionary behind a successful enterprise.

2) You are very in touch emotionally with those close to you. You are able to make new relationships quickly. You are also very psychic and intuitive in your relationships.

3) Your psychic insight and sensitivity synchronize you with your work.

4) You have great sensitivity to another's feelings. This can lead to strong emotional ties, but it can also repel or frighten others.

5) Great financial opportunities are available and must be acted upon. Don't procrastinate.

6) Go with your own intuition, but be careful about moving too soon.

7) Let your inner voice guide you in your personal life. The changes you seek can only come from within.

8) The success of your present venture depends on how much you work for it. Intuitive insight alone will not be enough.

9) Regarding your proposed venture, beware of building "castles in the air." Goals that cannot be achieved waste your time and energy.

10) The reaction to your idea will be based on intuition or insight. There may be suggestions about how to establish a firmer base.

11) Add the power of psychic energy to your thoughts. You can achieve your goal by visualizing and affirming it.

12) Trust your intuitive reaction. Don't swing on a star unless it's firmly anchored.

13) Seek an imaginative, aware individual, a visionary with hopes and dreams.

14) You are thought of as a sensitive and intuitive individual who has a tendency toward flights of fancy.

15) The answer to your question is "yes," but be careful of what you ask for because you may get it.

GREY

1) At present, it's unclear. There is too much confusion surrounding you at this time. Wait until things settle down, then ask the oracle again.

2) Your relationships are in a great deal of confusion and turmoil.

3) Your present career is surrounded by confusion because it lacks direction. You must decide where you belong.

4) There is confusion between you and your partner. It must be clarified before you can proceed.

5) At the present time, your financial forecast is too clouded to predict.

6) You're at an impasse in your career.

7) You must clear up all lingering doubts about your personal life.

8) The outcome of your present venture is uncertain.

9) Your proposed venture needs more clarification. If you start with confusion, it leads nowhere.

10) Your idea will not be viewed clearly. Expect delays or confusion.

11) Clear your thoughts. Energy should not be placed where there is no clarity.

12) Prospects of a new relationship are clouded. You need to work out your own problems first.

13) Until you decide what you really want, the type of person you should look for isn't clear.

14) There is a smoke screen surrounding your essential nature.

15) The answer to your question can't be answered with a "yes" or "no"—only a strong "maybe."

WHITE

1) You would do well in a career you believe will lead to truth and understanding, particularly ones that need the emotions put aside. Possibilities include scientist, judge, and psychiatrist, as well as such medical fields as doctor, lab technician, nurse, or any medical specialist.

2) You have a tendency to be standoffish and emotionally detached with friends and family.

3) Your understanding and wisdom are greatly appreciated by those who work closely with you. You bring clarity to all that you undertake.

4) The outlook is positive, but be a bit more emotional with your friend.

5) Your clear thinking and understanding should assure you a positive financial outlook.

6) The only changes are those that lead to enlightenment and understanding.

7) Understanding is the key to achieving a harmonious personal life.

8) Your present venture will lead to truth and enlightenment no matter what the outcome.

9) Your proposed venture, which means so much now, may take on a different meaning in the future. It could go either way.

10) The response to your idea will be positive, but do not expect great enthusiasm.

11) Look inward. Understanding the self is the basis of all understanding.

12) Your prospects for a new relationship are in the process of clearing. Don't be in a hurry to start again. First finish what you have started.

13) Look for an independent person, one who will not cling.

14) You are viewed as an understanding person, although somewhat unemotional.

15) The answer to your question is "yes," providing you can detach yourself from your emotions to obtain a better understanding.

BLACK

1) You have the ability to be what you want to be, but guard against negative thoughts. You may fit well in careers dealing with things that are hidden from the public, such as private investigator, occultist, or agent in the CIA, FBI, or other intelligence-gathering organization.

2) Your friendships are hidden from outside scrutiny. Others may see you as secretive and hard to approach.

3) There are hidden factors surrounding your career. An answer at this moment would be premature.

4) Hiding your emotions makes for one-sided relationships that lead to dead ends.

5) Do not accept all that is being shown to you. Hidden or unseen aspects are influencing your financial future. Seek out additional information.

6) The changes are not revealed, but there may be surprises ahead.

7) You need to open up to intimacy, and learn to share.

8) There is a possibility of a hidden, negative outcome regarding your present venture.

9) There are hidden aspects that make a final answer premature. Time will tell whether or not your proposed venture will succeed.

10) The response to your idea will be negative, and you may have to revise your ideas.

11) Expand your thinking by being open-minded. Examine what you've been keeping hidden.

12) There are no immediate prospects for a new relationship.

13) This is not the time to look for a new partner. Seek and you will not find.

14) There is a barrier between the two of you that can't be penetrated at this time.

15) The answer to your question is "no."

RAINBOW

1) Your adaptability, diversity, and versatility make you good at anything you do. The oracle suggests finding a job that is a challenge. Stay away from dull routines.

2) You are generally liked by all, although you may be considered a little hard to get close to.

3) Your adaptability makes your job a pathway to success.

4) Your relationship can be whatever you want it to be, but make sure it's what you want.

5) You're a go-getter. You're on the right path, and it leads you to your pot of gold.

6) There is always a possibility of change in anything you do, but your present career is moving ahead.

7) You change so readily that there is no need to concern yourself about it.

8) Stay on your present path with your present venture. It could lead to success.

9) Putting all your energy into your proposed venture will have a positive result.

10) As long as you present your ideas clearly, they will be well met.

11) Have faith in yourself. By knowing yourself well, you will go a long way.

12) You're a butterfly in the garden of life. You attract many people. Let it be known you are looking for a meaningful relationship.

13) Look for someone with a bright and sunny disposition with many and varied interests—a person you can talk to. As long as you can communicate, you'll never be bored.

14) He or she can see your diversity and adaptability and will respect it.

15) Yes.

5
FOUR-COLOR
RAINBOW READING

THIS METHOD OF COLOR divination will offer you a more detailed answer to your question, one that takes into account the influences surrounding your inquiry, the obstacles you face, the situation in the past, and the future outcome.

You should ask questions that call for an immediate answer or action. You're dealing with the near future, rather than a matter coming about over an extended period of time. As a general rule, the four-color Rainbow Reading is the best method to use whenever the situation you're evaluating is one in which you're asking, "What's going to happen now?" or "What should I do now?"

For example, if you're concerned about a change of residency, you might ask, "How will things work out with my plans to move?" Such a question addresses the present or the immediately upcoming situation. If you want to know how things will work out in the coming months—for example, six months into the future—you should use the six-color Rainbow Reading.

HOW TO WORD YOUR QUESTIONS

Pay close attention to the wording you use in your questions. Be conscious of nuances in the meaning. For example, notice the differences in the following questions, all of which relate to "my relationship with Joe":

1) "What should I do to improve the situation with Joe?"
2) "What does Joe think of me?"
3) "What's the outlook for my relationship with Joe?"

All these questions deal with a concern about the relationship with Joe, but each one is stated with a slightly different emphasis. What this means is that the oracle will provide a different answer to each of these questions, even if the exact same color is rolled. For example, if red appeared in the Outcome position, here are the answers with their different shades of meaning:

1) The oracle suggests you put more energy into the relationship.

2) Joe would react heatedly to you.

3) The outlook for the relationship is highly passionate.

Each question was answered by the color red, but the meanings were quite distinct.

Whenever the answer you receive to a question is completely unclear or confusing to you—not just an answer you don't want to hear—restate your question in a different way, and roll again. Don't just repeat the same question. That would only confuse matters, because the oracle's first response is always the right one. Since the wording is so important, it's a good idea to keep a journal of your Rainbow Readings, and write and rewrite your question until it says exactly what you want to know. Note the date of your Rainbow Reading, and also list the colors you rolled in each position.

THE POSITIONS

Each roll of the cubes represents a different aspect of your question, which corresponds to one of the four possible positions in your answer.

1. Surrounding influence
2. Obstacles faced
3. Past
4. Outcome

FIRST POSITION—INFLUENCES SURROUNDING THE QUESTION.

The Surrounding Influences refer to all the indirect effects upon the situation. These are the environmental factors. For example, if you're posing a question about whether or not you should ask for a raise, some of the Surrounding Influences would be how long ago you received your last raise, the financial status of the company, your employer's opinion of your work.

SECOND POSITION—OBSTACLES FACED.

This position refers to the challenges you face, or whatever is blocking you from achieving your goal. In the above example, the Obstacle could be the fact that your supervisor knows you'd be making almost as much as he or she makes if your raise were approved.

THIRD POSITION—THE PAST.

The concern here is whatever occurred in the past that is

playing a role in the matter at hand. In the example cited above, the fact that you won a major contract for your company a couple of months ago would no doubt play in your favor.

FOURTH POSITION—THE OUTCOME.

This position tells the upcoming result foreseen by your question. If you don't like the answer you receive, rolling again won't solve things. The first answer is always the right one. The best way to change an Outcome is by facing and overcoming the identified obstacles. For example, if the response to a request for a raise appears to indicate you won't get it, consider what you must do to qualify for a raise.

THE ROLL OF THE CUBES

When you begin a Rainbow Reading, hold all the cubes in your hand, take a few deep breaths, and center yourself. Focus on your question, or your wish for guidance, during the entire process of rolling the color cubes. For each position in the readings, roll the color cubes around in your hand for a moment and—without looking—choose one. Take the selected cube, shake it in your hand for a moment, then roll it out, just as though you were playing at dice. The color that lands face up is the color for that position. Write down the position and the colors rolled. Then—and this is very important—return all five cubes to your hand for each position to be rolled, and repeat the selection process.

If two cubes happen to fall out of your hand instead of just one, that's an additional message from the oracle. Read both the colors that turn up in that fashion for the selected position in the Rainbow Reading. For example, if red and silver slip from your hand as you prepare for your first roll, record both as Surrounding Influences, and interpret each of them. You'll probably discover that what seemed to be an "accidental" slip was not so accidental, and not without meaning.

HOW TO INTERPRET
FOUR-COLOR RAINBOW READINGS

The interpretations of the colors for the four- and six-cube Rainbow Readings will be found in Chapter 7. The interpretations include a brief summary of the meaning of the color called the *color key*, followed by three answer categories: the *Emotional*, the *Material*, and the *Spiritual*. Before you can begin to interpret your reading, you need to determine which of these categories is the appropriate one for your question.

If the question deals with relationships or personal feelings or attitudes, the Emotional category is the appropriate answer section. If the question is related to money, business, finances, career, or anything related to material goods or concerns, the section labeled Material should be consulted. For all questions related to one's inner search, highest goals, spiritual quest, or life purpose, refer to the section labeled Spiritual.

Some questions involve more than one category. For example, if your question involves both a relationship and your career, you would consult the Emotional and Material categories.

SAMPLE READINGS

Before you begin casting your first four-color Rainbow Readings, it's important to practice interpreting the meanings of various colors. To help you with interpretation, we're offering you the following sample readings as examples. But also remember, practice is essential if you are to avoid confusion when you begin to do your own readings.

Start by reading the introduction to the sample readings. Each one ends with the question asked, and is followed by a notation of the appropriate answer category—Emotional, Material, or Spiritual. Then, turn to Chapter 7 and find the color mentioned. First, read the color key; then find the appropriate answer category, and read the general meaning as well as the specific meanings related to the position in which the color fell.

For example, for the first sample reading, which concerns Tony, a retired accountant, turn to page 103 to locate your First Position answer—Red (Intensified). Read the color key, then find the Material category and read the first paragraph. Then below it, read the Surrounding Influences, which is what the First Position represents. Next, move on to the Second Position, turning to page 127 for Blue (Intensified). Read the color key. Refer to the Material category again, and find the Obstacle, the interpretation for the Second Position. As you flip back and forth between the interpretations and the sample readings, you'll begin to see how the color interpretations are applied to the specific concerns these people expressed in their questions.

All these examples are taken from actual Rainbow Readings conducted in 1987 and the first few months of 1988. The participants' questions and comments about the readings are recounted exactly as they were told.

TONY, 72, RETIRED ACCOUNTANT

BACKGROUND: When Tony retired six years ago, he invested some of his savings in two parcels of commercial property along a main highway on the west coast of Florida. He's been waiting for this area to develop, but little has happened. As a result, for the past year he's been trying to sell the properties but has found no takers.

QUESTION: "What's the outlook for selling the Florida property?"

ANSWER CATEGORY: Material.

First Position—Surrounding Influences: Red (Intensified).

Color Keys: Anxiety. Great stress.

Tony's concern about money matters is creating stressful circumstances, to the point where finances are ruling his life instead of allowing him to enjoy life.

Second Position—Obstacles Faced: Blue (Intensified).

Color Keys: Isolation.

The Obstacle Tony's facing deals with isolation. The property is located at a considerable distance from the nearest area of commercial development. This isolated locale is making the two land parcels difficult to sell. The oracle's suggestion is to focus on a positive aspect, and use that as a basis for change.

TONY'S COMMENTS: Recently he said he's been thinking about putting more effort into selling the smaller parcel of land, rather than trying to sell both parcels at the same time.

Third Position—Past: Purple.
Color Keys: The Past. Rules and regulations.

Tony's situation is tied to the past—in other words, his past purchase of the land six years ago. He would like to take a long trip with his wife, but he feels he's not in the financial position to do so until he sells the land. Thus, the land, in a sense, has become a restriction for Tony—he's fallen into a rut.

Fourth Position—Outcome: Green.
Color Keys: Change. Growth. Money.

The oracle foresaw a favorable advancement in the matter at hand. It indicated that money was coming, but not necessarily a large sum.

CONCLUSION: The oracle proved correct. Tony advertised the smaller piece of property and sold it several weeks later, alleviating the immediate financial crunch.

JORGE, 43, HOTELIER

BACKGROUND: Jorge is from a family that owns several hotels in South America. He's in the process of buying a hotel in Miami Beach, and several Latin American investors are helping him. However, Jorge's been having some problems with the other investors, and he was interested in finding out if everything would go smoothly.

QUESTION: "What's the outlook for completing the deal?" (This question concerns both relationships and business matters, so it is best interpreted using both the Emotional and Material categories.)

ANSWER CATEGORY: Emotional and Material.

First Position—Surrounding Influences: Green.

Color Keys: Change. Growth. Money.

Green as a Surrounding Influence in the Emotional category speaks of a change. It suggests a new relationship affecting the matter of concern.

Under the Material category, it suggests that Jorge has had a change of mind regarding his plans. Everything is changing.

JORGE'S COMMENTS: "I've had these difficulties with my investors. They keep changing their minds. It's caused some frustrating times for me."

Second Position—Obstacles Faced: Purple (Intensified).

Color Keys: Restrictions. Narrow-minded thinking. Rigidly tied to the past.

Your ties to the past are holding you down. You may be making the same mistakes you made in the past. Instead of opening new doors, you are building barriers around you. (Material.)

There is no free flow of thoughts and feelings in your relationship. It is stifling for one or both of you. You are bound by numerous restrictions. (Emotional.)

JORGE'S COMMENTS: "That's exactly it. I feel the other investors are restricting me."

Third Position—Past: Purple.

Color Keys: Tradition. The past. Rules and regulations.

With purple in the Past position, the oracle suggests that you have dealt with the structures of rules and regulations, leaving little room for anything new. (Material.)

Your relationships could not progress beyond past rules and restrictions. (Emotional.)

JORGE'S COMMENTS: "You see my situation now. These

ties from the past are what I need to make the hotel work. But at the same time, they're what's blocking me from doing things the way I want to do them."

Fourth Position—Outcome: Orange (Intensified).

Color Keys: Irrational thought. Overemotional or overly logical.

You're trying to force matters to come out the way that you want them; you're counteracting the natural balance. Consequently, you feel out of sync in your relationship. (Emotional.)

You're putting the wrong emphasis on what you think you want and what it is you really want. The oracle suggests that you balance this out. You may be entering a career or business venture for all the wrong reasons. (Material.)

JORGE'S COMMENTS: "There may be some truth there. The imbalance is between me and my investors. The fact is I may be putting too much emphasis on the hotel as my personal power base. That concerns the others, because even though they are not here, they are also owners."

CONCLUSION: Jorge made adjustments in the plan and harmonized his relationship with his business partners. Within three months, he had worked out the details to the satisfaction of the investors and purchased the Miami Beach hotel. He successfully altered the Outcome foreseen by achieving the necessary balance.

SUSAN ASKING ABOUT BILL, REAL ESTATE AGENT, AGE 35

BACKGROUND: The inquirer, Susan, had a question about her divorced brother, Bill, who had been looking for a romantic involvement for some time. She was planning on introducing

Bill to an attractive young woman named Ellen, who would be coming to a party at her house. Ellen was very involved in exploring psychic realms, and the evening was going to include an experiment in hypnotic regression into past lives. Bill had little interest in the subject, and thought people who did might not have a firm grip on reality.

QUESTION: "What are the chances for a romance developing between Bill and Ellen?"

ANSWER CATEGORY: Emotional.

First Position—Surrounding Influences: Pink.

Color Keys: Gentle love. Tenderness. Sensitivity.

As a Surrounding Influence, pink suggests there is love in the air. The circumstances look promising for romance.

Second Position—Obstacles Faced: Violet.

Color Keys: Spirituality. Idealism.

The Obstacle faced is Ellen's interest in spirituality. Her fascination with spiritual matters could block the development of the relationship. The oracle suggests that both Bill and Ellen may find fault with anyone who's not up to their standards. Bill must avoid any rigidly skeptical stance, and Ellen must come down to Earth.

Third Position—Past: Gold.

Color Keys: Positive thinking. Success.

Bill is coming into the situation with a positive attitude. If he is interested in Ellen, she will very likely respond in a positive way.

Fourth Position—Outcome: Brown.

Color Keys: Solid foundations. A fertile time.

As an Outcome, brown holds the promise of a relationship taking root. If Bill and Ellen make the effort, the Obstacle could be overcome, and a stable relationship built on a solid foundation could evolve.

SUSAN'S COMMENTS: A few days after the party, Susan reported the following: "I noticed Bill and Ellen stealing looks at each other during the evening. They sat next to each other at a table for a while and Bill seemed to be attracted to Ellen, especially after she mentioned early on that she had recently ended a two-year relationship with a man. But the talk of 'karma' and other spiritual matters kept Bill on the fringes of the conversation most of the night. Yet, after Ellen left, Bill casually asked a couple of questions about her, and when we talked a couple of days later he said he'd like to see Ellen again, but he never called her up."

CONCLUSION: This reading is a good example of how free will can affect the end result of any reading. While the reading showed a favorable possibility, Bill wavered and chose not to overcome the obstacles. As a result of his nonaction, the potential relationship never took root.

GRETCHEN, INTERIOR DECORATOR, AGE 27

Gretchen is a quiet, intense young woman who doesn't hide the fact that she's seeking direction in her life.

QUESTION: "What changes should I make in my life?"

ANSWER CATEGORY: Emotional.

First Position—Surrounding Influences: Green.

Color Keys: Change. Growth. Renewal. New ideas.

As a Surrounding Influence, green suggests that the desire for emotional growth, possibly a new relationship or the expansion of an existing one, is affecting the matter you are asking about.

GRETCHEN'S COMMENTS: "The color keys, I think, accurately describe my situation. I'm working on changing, renewing myself. I've been involved in a relationship for eight years that I want to end now. I want to get past it."

Second Position—Obstacles Faced: Pink (Intensified).

Color Keys: Loss of vitality. Lack of love.

The loss of vitality or the lack of love in your life is blocking you from accomplishing your goal of emotional growth and a new relationship.

GRETCHEN'S COMMENTS: "I've been seeing a counselor who's been helping me understand how my present relationship is related to my childhood experiences. There was a lack of love in my family. My mother was cold, and my father didn't show his love. I was always ashamed, told that I wasn't worth anything. I guess all of that is the obstacle I face in finding my direction."

Third Position—Past: Black.

Color Keys: Hidden thoughts, feelings, or actions. Something that's not presently being revealed.

AUTHOR'S COMMENTS: This cube slipped out of Gretchen's hand as she was shaking the cubes. Although she mentioned her interest in ending her eight-year relationship, she didn't say why. That was the element she preferred keeping hidden. Later, it turned out that the relationship was entwined with a drug problem.

Fourth Position—Outcome: Gold.

Color Keys: Creative thought. Attainment of goals. Positive thinking.

In the Outcome position, the oracle suggests that Gretchen's desires for emotional growth will be fulfilled.

AUTHOR'S COMMENTS: The oracle forecast success for Gretchen *if* she continued in her current pursuits with a positive attitude. The circumstances influencing her are growth and rebirth. But first she must deal with her past. When she clears away the matters that are bothering her and approaches the future with a positive sense, she'll attain her goal of revitalizing herself.

CONCLUSION: Within a couple of months, Gretchen entered a drug rehabilitation program and underwent substantial changes in her personal life. As a result, she did indeed have a better outlook than at the time she asked the question.

6
SIX-COLOR
RAINBOW READING

This FORECAST METHOD
goes beyond the four-color reading in that it provides a six-month forecast rather than focusing on the situation currently developing. Your question for a six-color Rainbow Reading should be time-related. You want to find out what's in store over the next six months, or what you should be doing over that period to achieve a goal.

For example, if your concern is a career matter, you might ask: "What is the outlook for taking a new job?" Strive to be specific. Instead of saying: "What direction will my life take in the next six months?" rephrase your question and frame it within a specific area of your life, such as career or personal goals. A more specific version of asking what's in store might be—"What direction will my romantic life take in the next six months?"

Keep in mind that the oracle may be indicating a direction or path you are now setting up for yourself at an unconscious level. If you don't like what lies ahead, you have the power to avert it. The advantage six-color Rainbow Readings give you is that you will have a better idea of your direction.

The more you know, the better prepared you are for changes.

As with the four-color method, it's a good practice to write down your question in your Rainbow Journal. Then, hold the cubes and relax yourself. Think about your question, or your wish for guidance, while you're rolling the color cubes. For each of the six positions in the readings, roll the color cubes around in your hand for a moment and—without looking—choose one, shake it in your hand for a moment, then roll it out, just as though you were playing at dice. The color that lands uppermost is the color for that position. Write down the position and the color rolled. Then—and this is very important—return all five cubes to your hand for each position to be rolled, and repeat the selection process until all six color positions are filled.

If two cubes happen to fall out of your hand instead of just one, that's an additional message from the oracle. Read both the colors that turn up for the selected position in the Rainbow Reading.

Here are the designations of the six positions, starting with the first roll:

1. Surrounding influences
2. Obstacle
3. Past
4. Present
5. Future (1–3 months)
6. Future (4–6 months)

The first three positions are the same as the positions cast in the four-color method. In addition, the fourth position deals with the Present, while the fifth and sixth positions deal with the near Future—one to three months—and the more distant Future—four to six months.

To assist you with interpretations, we've included several sample readings. Turn to Chapter 7, on color interpretations, and follow along so you can see how the interpretation was made. For example, Delores, the bridge player, rolled the color green in Position One, Surrounding Influences. Begin by reading the color key, then go to the section on the Material, and read the first paragraph. Then find the sentence or sentences addressing the appropriate position: the Surrounding Influences. Do the same for the Second Position roll, and so on.

SAMPLE READINGS

DELORES, AGE 65, BRIDGE PLAYER

BACKGROUND: Bridge is a passion with Delores. She not only plays bridge regularly, but also teaches the game. She was interested in finding out what lay ahead for her bridge career.
QUESTION: "What's in store for me in the next six months in my bridge career?"
ANSWER CATEGORY: Material.
First Position—Surrounding Influences: Green.
Color Keys: Growth. Change. New ideas.

An advancement or change in Delores's bridge career may be impending. She may have had a change in plans. Everything around her bridge career is changing. Growth is indicated.

DELORES'S COMMENTS: "I've been thinking some about teaching bridge on a cruise ship. It's probably a good time for it, but I'm not so sure I want to bother with it."

Second Position—Obstacles Faced: White/Orange.

Color Keys: (White) Understanding reached through clear and positive thinking. Insightful awareness. Protection. (Orange) Harmony. Balance between the mind and emotions.

Two cubes slipped out of Delores's hand. The combination means that she needs to understand how to balance her mind and emotions. (See Chapter 8: Color Combinations.)

DELORES'S COMMENTS: "That's exactly the problem I have with my game. My temperament is my biggest obstacle. I tend to get upset with my partner. I'll get distracted, and lose the hand."

Third Position—Past: Purple.

Color Keys: Tradition. The past. Rules and regulations.

In the past, Delores's bridge playing has been bound by certain rules and regulations—it did not progress beyond the rules and regulations.

DELORES'S COMMENTS: "I'm not always willing to take chances when I should. I guess in a way I've been bound by my own rules and regulations regarding my play."

Fourth Position—Present: Violet.

Color Keys: The highest order of anything.

The oracle indicates that you've achieved the highest order of what you've set out to achieve. Delores is a Life Master of bridge, the game's highest designation. Any lesser achievement would be unfulfilling.

Fifth Position—Future (One to Three Months): Brown.

Color Keys: Solid foundations. A fertile time.

Delores has a solid foundation of experience. She is likely to achieve all she sets out to do in her game. If she wanted to teach the game on cruise ships she would have little difficulty in making arrangements, and the benefits might be greater than expected.

Sixth Position—Future (Four to Six Months): Peach.
Color Keys: Balance. Happiness.

The oracle signifies that by following the path she's on in her bridge career, Delores will achieve happiness and balance.

RENIE, 49-YEAR-OLD FREELANCE COMMERCIAL ARTIST

BACKGROUND: For the past couple of years, Renie has been working full-time for one client. Recently, she's been planning to start a marketing and public relations business with a partner.

QUESTION: "What's coming up in the next six months regarding my career?"

ANSWER CATEGORY: Material.

First Position—Surrounding Influences: Red (Intensified).

Color Keys: Anxiety. Great stress. Anger. Fear.

The oracle indicates that Renie's career is surrounded by extreme stress. There's a need to evaluate the situation closely. If you've become obsessive about the issue, you need to step back and look at it from a distance. Intense feelings are blocking your thinking.

RENIE'S COMMENTS: "I've been trying to quit that job twice a week for the last two months. I've been a hostile, antagonistic bitch, and I go home literally gnawing at the steering wheel."

Second Position—Obstacles Faced: Green (Intensified).

Color Keys: Deceit. Treachery. Duplicity. Envy. Unnecessary change.

You're bouncing around too much. You're being side-tracked, making too many changes. If you take too many paths, it usually leads to blind alleys. Think twice about the changes you're making.

RENIE'S COMMENTS: "I've been trying hard to bring the company I'm working with into the modern era of advertising and marketing, and I've been getting lots of grief for all the changes I'm trying to make. It's been costly for me: a pound of flesh for every step forward."

Third Position—Past: Brown.

Color Keys: Solid foundations. Security. Stability.

In the Past position, brown reveals that a firm foundation was laid in an earlier time. The indication is that in the past her job served as a source of security and stability.

RENIE'S COMMENTS: "When I took on this client, I did so because I needed the financial security that the company could provide. It gave me the stability I needed—a regular paycheck."

Fourth Position—Present: Green.

Color Keys: Change. Growth. Money. New ideas.

An advancement or change in your career may be impending. There may be a modest raise or financial gain in the offing. Regarding business matters, the time is ripe for putting a new idea into motion, or expanding on an existing one. A change for the better is in motion. Don't worry.

AUTHOR'S COMMENTS: While Renie was shaking the cubes, she twice dropped one of them and green turned up both times. Although she was told she should use it, she said that she was looking at another person in the room who was talking at the time. When she did finally roll, to her surprise, green turned up again.

RENIE'S COMMENTS: "A change in my career is exactly what I've been planning. I have an opportunity to start a new business, and I'm thinking seriously about it."

Fifth Position—Future (One to Three Months): Yellow/Green.
Color Keys: (See Other Significant Combinations in Chapter 8, p. 169.) Legal change. Marriage. Divorce. Change of residence. Change of job.

AUTHOR'S COMMENTS: As Renie shook the cubes in her hand, two of them fell out, yellow on the left, green on the right. This time, she accepted the accidental roll.

The yellow/green combination is one of the most significant. It denotes legal change. In the Material category, it could mean a pending contract, a change of residence, or a new job.

RENIE'S COMMENTS: "I have a financial backer for my new business, but at present we haven't signed any contract or financial agreement."

Sixth Position—Future (Four to Six Months): White.
Color Keys: Realization. Protection. Understanding reached through clear and positive thinking.

The road ahead is clear and positive. Renie will have the understanding to achieve whatever she wants.

RENIE'S COMMENTS: "Even though I very much want this new business idea to work, I don't want to to be tied down by it. I guess, you *could* say, I want to be able to stand apart from it. That's the advantage of working freelance. You have more flexibility and control."

CONCLUSION: Renie wasn't completely satisfied with the answer she received from the Future position. She asked for a clarification by throwing another cube to use in combination with white. A blue cube turned up. The white/blue combination means: You need to seek understanding through your inner self.

RENIE'S COMMENTS: "I guess I haven't really thought everything through. It seems to be saying that I should think more on exactly what I want. One of my options is opening the business here in South Florida, or taking it out west to Arizona. I haven't decided yet."

Finally, Renie decided to use the one-cube method as a follow-up, and ask how she would do with the business if she stayed in South Florida—Question 9. Orange turned up: Success is likely in your proposed venture. Then she asked how she'd do if she moved—Question 9 again. She rolled a red cube: Your proposed venture needs to be examined more closely to avoid stress.

RENIE'S COMMENTS: "If I did move, I'd be very dependent on other people until the business got off the ground. I'm not sure I'm ready for that."

ALISON, A 40-YEAR-OLD MYSTERY WRITER

BACKGROUND: At the time she rolled the cubes, Alison was working on her second novel.

QUESTION: "What's the outlook on the book over the next six months?"

ANSWER CATEGORY: Emotional and Material. (Since a mystery novel deals with the emotional realm as well as the material, the interpretations were drawn from both sections.)

First Position—Surrounding Influences: Green.

Color Keys: Change. Growth. New ideas.

The oracle indicates that Alison is a changeable person, who looks ahead and wants to grow. It suggests a new relationship or a revitalization of an existing one in regard to her book. (Emotional.)

Green as a Surrounding Influence suggests a change of mind regarding one's plans. Growth is indicated. (Material.)

ALISON'S COMMENTS: "The book features a serial character, a female cop, who appeared in my first mystery. In this book I'm expanding on her character, getting to know her better. I guess you could say I'm revitalizing an old friendship with a new perspective."

Second Position—Obstacles Faced: Blue.

Color Keys: Tranquility. Sensitivity. Introverted. Private.

In this position, it appears that your reticence is blocking you—you're keeping your feelings inside. You need to break out of your shell. (Emotional.)

You're being too complacent and being lulled by a false sense of security. (Material.)

ALISON'S COMMENTS: "This was tough to figure out at

first. There is a sense of tranquility and privacy about writing a book, but I don't consider it an Obstacle. What I think it means is that I'm working inside my head now. No one but me has read any of the book, and I view that as an Obstacle. I haven't had a second opinion. I'll break out of my shell when I let someone else read it."

Third Position—Past: Red (Intensified).

Color Keys: Anxiety. Great stress. Anger. Fear. Obsession.

A relationship may have become a hostile love affair that could involve sadomasochism, physical abuse, or vendettas. The relationship is so intense that it's consuming itself. Extreme feelings of anger, passion, fear, and anxiety play a role in this book. (Emotional/Material.)

ALISON'S COMMENTS: "The book is about a vendetta. That's what I've been writing about. All those emotions— anger, passion, fear, anxiety—are what the murderer is feeling."

Fourth Position—Present: Red (Intensified).

Color Keys: Anxiety. Great stress. Anger. Fear. Obsession.

In the Present position, anger, stress, or extreme passion is affecting your ability to see clearly. You need a fresh perspective. In this case, the near Past and the Present are both red intensified. Both answers relate to the feelings expressed by the characters in the book. However, if the writing of the book is causing stress, take a break. Instead of confronting the situation head-on, which is the tendency here, sidestep it. The advice of the oracle is that change would be for the better because your circumstances are rife with stress.

Fifth Position—Future (One to Three Months): Brown.

Color Keys: Solid foundations. A fertile time.

A sound emotional foundation is forming and will be realized. (Emotional.)

The oracle indicates you can expect to achieve whatever you are seeking with unexpected benefits. (Material.)

ALISON'S COMMENTS: "I feel the story is taking root. I feel good about it."

Sixth Position—Future (Three to Six Months): Pink.

Color Keys: Love. Health. Vitality.

The future is bright. (Emotional.)

The outlook for the book is healthy. Continue on your course. (Material.)

CONCLUSION: Three months after completing the book, and five months after the reading, Alison received a multi-book contract.

JENINE, ADMINISTRATIVE ASSISTANT

BACKGROUND: A resident of a medium-sized Midwestern city, this 24-year-old woman works in city government. Jenine said she was a skeptic, and expressed little faith that a divinatory tool based on color could tell her anything about herself. She only participated because of the encouragement of two friends who both work with her.

QUESTION: "What's the outlook for my career over the next six months?"

ANSWER CATEGORY: Material.

First Position—Surrounding Influences: Brown.

Color Keys: Security. Stability.

Jenine is looking for security in her career. Brown as a

Surrounding Influence indicates that she is greatly affected by what is firm and stable.

Second Position—Obstacles Faced: Grey.

Color Keys: Confusion. Misunderstanding. Fear.

As an Obstacle, grey indicates confusion. Until Jenine can think clearly, she shouldn't make any career decisions.

Third Position—Past: Red.

Color Keys: Heightened physical or emotional energy. Passion. Intensity.

Red in the Past position indicates that an emotionally charged matter from the past is affecting Jenine's career outlook.

Fourth Position—Present: Peach.

Color Keys: Balance. Mellowness. Happiness.

At present, things have calmed down, and are going well, and you should be happy about it. But keep your eyes open. Don't be overconfident. The situation could change.

Fifth Position—Future (One to Three Months): Silver.

Color Keys: Versatility. Intuition. Psychic awareness.

In the near future, Jenine should use her intuition when making career decisions. Once she learns to trust her psychic or intuitive insights, she will grow emotionally in regard to her career.

Sixth Position—Future (Four to Six Months): Orange (Intensified)/Violet.

Color Keys: (Orange Intensified) Imbalance. Irrational thought. Overemotional or overly logical. (Violet) The highest order of anything. Wisdom. Spirituality. Idealism.

Here again is an example where two cubes slipped out of

someone's hand. Both were used in the reading. The combination suggests that Jenine has set high goals for herself, but the course she is following to achieve them is irrational. She is either too emotional or too logical. Something is out of balance.

AUTHOR'S COMMENTS: Jenine remained smug and silent throughout the reading. She gave no indication of what she thought. However, after she left, her associates attested to its accuracy. They explained that Jenine has had difficulties with her boss and has been concerned about the security of her job. Things have calmed down lately, but only because she avoided overreacting to her boss's demands.

CONCLUSION: Jenine later told others she worked with about the experience, saying that none of it meant anything. She ignored the oracle's suggestions, which reflected her own unconscious mind's efforts to warn her. Four months later, Jenine was fired.

TOM, AGE 40, PHOTOGRAPHER

BACKGROUND: Although it's not something he talks about with many people, Tom is on a quest for higher knowledge. In the past, he's sampled a variety of consciousness-raising activities from meditation to yoga and Rolfing. Lately, the more mundane activities of daily living have overwhelmed him. Now he wonders what's in store for him.

QUESTION: "What's the six-month outlook regarding my spiritual search?"

ANSWER CATEGORY: Spiritual.

First Position—Surrounding Influences: Black.

Color Keys: Hidden thoughts, feelings, or actions. Something that's not presently being revealed.

Tom's search will be affected by something or someone now hidden from him.

Second Position—Obstacles Faced: Peach.

Color Keys: Balance. Mellowness. Happiness.

Tom will find joy through his search for higher meaning in life. The end results aren't as important as the steps one takes to get there. Often, spiritual gains are made in times of crisis. As an Obstacle, peach suggests that Tom's spiritual awakening is being slowed or blocked by his sense of complacency, caused by mellowness and contentment.

TOM'S COMMENTS: "Things are on an even keel for me. I'm busy working every day on projects. I suppose that balance does have a mellowing effect. A few years ago, I went through a period when everything was changing in my life. It was total chaos, but that was also a period when I felt I was making gains in my awareness. In all the chaos, remarkable things were happening that defy explanation. Whatever I needed came to me just at the right time."

Third Position—Past: Gold.

Color Keys: Success. Creative thought. Attainment of goals.

Success is the key word. Tom's positive thoughts and feelings in the past successfully advanced his spiritual quest.

Fourth Position—Present: Yellow (Intensified).

Color Keys: Illogical. Intellectual blocks. Skeptical or cynical attitudes.

You reduce everything to logic, even when logic doesn't apply. In the Present position, intensified yellow indicates that rigid thinking bound by logic has created barriers to spiritual growth. Review what you've learned and sort out the things that have confused you.

TOM'S COMMENTS: "I do have a tendency to look on most things in a logical vein. I always look for a cause and effect, even though I know at a deeper level that everything doesn't work that way."

Fifth Position—Future (One to Three Months): Brown.
Color Keys: Solid foundations. A fertile time.

You put your higher consciousness to use in your everyday activities. You are able to function and make use of it in all your endeavors. You will remain well rooted in any spiritual undertaking. You won't get lost in the clouds.

Sixth Position—Future (Four to Six Months): Green.
Color Keys: Growth. Healing. Renewal. New ideas.

Growth, expansion, and renewal are indicated in Tom's spiritual quest. Since green is the color of healing, it could indicate the beginning of a personal transformation or a new world opening in your spiritual quest. Expect enlightenment and understanding in what you seek. As you grow, the barriers around you will dissolve. You might consider delving into the healing arts.

CONCLUSION: Several months later, Tom was shown the reading and asked what he thought.

"About three weeks after the reading, I was hired by a magazine for a well-paying but rather mundane project. However, the contact has led to another project. In a couple of months I'll be going to South America to photograph the ceremonies of an Indian tribe which still maintains primitive rituals. I'm not sure, but some of them may involve the healing arts. Anyhow, to prepare for the assignment, I've been reading everything I can get my hands on about American Indian rituals. It's already opened some interesting doors, especially regarding the Native American ideas on balancing the positive and negative, the dark and light, to achieve spiritual harmony."

7
INTERPRETATIONS:
FOUR-COLOR AND SIX-COLOR
RAINBOW READINGS

Each color interpretation begins with a list of color keys—words which unlock the meaning of a color in a few words. The color keys are followed by sections labeled the Emotional, Material, and Spiritual. Under each heading is a paragraph or two describing the general nature of the color as it pertains to the specific category. Following that are the specifics: what the color means when it is rolled as a surrounding influence; as an obstacle; in the past; in the present. The outcome and the two future positions are grouped together.

Say your question was: "What is the outlook for my spiritual quest?" (The last example in Chapter 6.) You're throwing a six-cube rainbow reading, and you want to interpret the Obstacle position in which you rolled the color peach. You would turn to the section on Peach, and find the category of Spiritual. After reading over the general material, you would refer to the specific sentence or sentences on peach as an obstacle.

The interpretations for the intensified colors—the darker tones signified with diagonal white slashes—follow the interpretation of the color in its normal hue. In general, the intensified colors represent the extremes of a situation. For example, red pertains to high energy and passion, and the intensified red deals with the point where high energy bubbles over into stress and anxiety—or the extreme experience of high energy or passion.

Take your time interpreting the meanings of the colors after you cast your readings. It's important to develop a clear understanding of the meaning of each color and how it relates to the position and category of your question.

At first, you may experience some frustrations in interpreting the four- and six-color readings. Terms like *position* and *category* can be confusing when first presented. However, once you're familiar with the method, you'll be able to quickly find the appropriate section in the interpretations. Then the fun begins. No doubt, you'll soon experience a reading that is uncanny in its accuracy, almost as if the message was written directly to you. That's when you know that the magic of the oracle is flowing through you.

RED

COLOR KEYS: Passion. Intensity. Ardent enthusiasm. Heightened physical and emotional energy.

EMOTIONAL

Red is a color of high emotion, sometimes to the point that logical considerations are overlooked. In terms of relationships, red indicates a high-pitched, intense union. In romantic affairs, passion is the key word. The partners have strong feelings about each other. To maintain your relationship, it's important to balance your emotions with logic, and reach an understanding about what each of you want out of the relationship.

❑ If you rolled red in the first position, Surrounding Influences, it indicates that heightened energy or high passion is coloring your thinking.

❑ As an Obstacle, fiery emotions are interfering or blocking you. The oracle suggests you back off; let your emotions cool before any confrontation occurs.

❑ In the Past position, red reveals that an emotionally charged matter from the past is affecting the concern.

❑ In the Present position, red indicates that a highly emotional state is at the heart of the matter now.

❑ As an Outcome or in one of the Future positions, red suggests that the matter under question will result in high emotions, or a passionate encounter.

MATERIAL

You may be experiencing periods of high energy that

can be successfully channeled into your work, as long as you guard against burning yourself out. Your energy level powers you along, but be cautious of making hasty, impetuous decisions. Seek balance. If you're being pressed for a decision, set the matter aside for a few days and then return to it.

Red as a material factor may also indicate an obsession with finances, and this creates stressful situations. You need to stop and allow things to happen, rather than driving yourself so hard. Keep in mind that everything happens in its own time, and you can't always force what you want to occur. Calm down and allow the fruits of your labor to blossom.

❏ If red appears as a Surrounding Influence, it suggests that high energy or a possibly explosive situation is influencing matters.

❏ As an Obstacle, red warns of stress. Don't overwork yourself.

❏ In the Past position, the color indicates that high energy was expended regarding the matter under question.

❏ In the Present position, red indicates that a surge of energy is driving you. Take advantage of it, but beware of stressful situations.

❏ As an Outcome or in a Future position, red suggests that the outlook is for a high-energy result. There will be plenty of energy and enthusiasm generated.

SPIRITUAL

Your unconscious mind is charged with high energy, usually triggered by emotion-evoking symbology. Your path to higher consciousness may involve rituals with physical movement leading to altered states of consciousness. Sufi dancing, gospel singing, fire walking, and trance channeling are a few examples. By taking advantage of the energy, and by keeping a positive perspective, much can be achieved. Without such high energy, many quests would not be undertaken. But once started, the energy generated moves quickly. You must know how to control it, and not allow it to control you.

❑ As a Surrounding Influence, red suggests the energy around the situation is intense.

❑ As an Obstacle, too much energy is being placed into the situation. There is a danger of losing control.

❑ In the Past position, high energy has fueled your quest. There has been little letup.

❑ In the Present position, red indicates that the unconscious mind is a powerhouse of energy.

❑ As an Outcome or in a Future position, red indicates that the energy you need will be available. Everything will move along rapidly on the path you are following.

RED (Intensified)

COLOR KEYS: Extreme passion. Anxiety. Great stress. Anger.
Fear. Obsession.

EMOTIONAL

Intensified red denotes extreme circumstances. In such a
situation there's a need to evaluate the situation closely. If
you've become obsessive about a matter, you need to step
back and look at it from a distance. Your intense feelings are
blocking your thinking.

In relationships, extreme passion may flare into jealousy,
violent anger, or stress. Instances of abusive behavior may be
followed by passionate lovemaking. The relationship may be
so intense that it's consuming itself. Ask yourself who, if anyone, is benefiting from the affair.

❑ As a Surrounding Influence, intensified red suggests
that circumstances related to your concern are causing extreme stress. Your feelings are out of control.

❑ As an Obstacle, you are being told that your extreme
emotions are blocking you from achieving your objective, or
from resolving a concern.

❑ In the Past position, intensified red suggests that extreme feelings of anger, passion, or fear played a role in your
situation. The oracle could be reminding you that what took
place before could occur again if you're not careful.

❑ In the Present position, anger, stress, or extreme passion is affecting your ability to see clearly. You need a fresh
perspective.

❑ As an Outcome or in a Future position, intensified red

warns that you may be facing situations with extreme stress if you continue to follow the path you are on or inquiring about.

MATERIAL

Extreme stress. Care should be taken to safeguard your mental and physical health. Seek alternatives for those areas of your life where the stress is greatest. If the source of stress is your job and you've been contemplating a vacation, then now is the time to take it. Instead of confronting the situation head-on, which is the tendency here, sidestep it. Remove yourself. The oracle suggests curbing aggressive tendencies.

As to finances, you may be experiencing great concern over money matters. Possibly, finances are ruling your life instead of allowing you to enjoy life.

❑ If intensified red appears as a Surrounding Influence, it indicates that extreme stress is affecting matters.

❑ As an Obstacle, intensified red suggests that stress is blocking you from moving ahead. Take the necessary steps to diffuse it.

❑ In the Past position, intensified red reveals that anxiety, fear, or stress have played a part in the matter that concerns you.

❑ In the Present position, intensified red indicates that a stressful situation is at hand. The advice of the oracle is that change would be for the better because your present circumstances are rife with stress.

❑ As an Outcome or in a Future position, intensified red warns that you are heading toward a situation of extreme stress unless you alter your course. Prepare for it, or avoid it, if possible.

SPIRITUAL

Your search for guidance has reached a point where you possess an obsessive allegiance to a cause or belief. The intensified red suggests a mind-set that is often characterized by the term *fire and brimstone*. You believe there is only one truth and everyone must adhere to it. Consider that the continued pursuit of such fanatical behavior could retard spiritual growth. The influence here would be the equivalent of the attitude that permeated the Crusades: war for religious causes.

❑ If intensified red appears in the Surrounding Influences position, it suggests the path of the person inquired about is influenced by an overzealousness bordering on fanatical belief. Once removed from the environment, the person would soon begin to question what had seemed so right before.

❑ As an Obstacle, intensified red means that obsessiveness is the cause of the impasse.

❑ In the Past position, this color shows that erratic behavior or beliefs have been a strong factor in the matter under question.

❑ In the Present position, you (or the person under consideration) have reached a point where the fact must be recognized that fanatical belief or behavior lies at the heart of the problem.

❑ Intensified red as an Outcome or in a Future position warns that the spiritual fire you are fanning may end up engulfing you. The oracle's advice: Change your ways.

ORANGE

COLOR KEYS: Harmony. Balance between the mind and emotions.

EMOTIONAL

You're seeking a balance in your life. There is a tempering of the emotional side with logic, and vice versa.

In a relationship, you add substance and direction to it by balancing emotional involvement with the intellect. You can see where it's headed. Since this is not a purely emotional relationship, the level of passion may not be intense. However, what starts slowly could develop into something more lasting with a firmer base. Sometimes we have to follow our heart, not logic.

☐ Orange as a Surrounding Influence signifies that the subject in question is being balanced. It can be seen on both levels—the emotional and the logical.

☐ As an Obstacle, orange indicates that the balancing of the mind and the emotions may not lead to what you desire. The oracle suggests that you follow your heart.

☐ In the Past position, orange reveals that there has been a balance of emotions and logic.

☐ In the Present position, the indication is that the matter under question has reached a point of harmony.

☐ As an Outcome or in a Future position, orange implies that a balance between the emotions and the intellect will be reached. The outlook appears harmonious.

MATERIAL

Balance your feelings with logic. Weigh carefully what you think and what you feel. Use that as a guide to advance yourself. You possess the abilities needed for success. In financial matters, you are your own best judge of the viability of your endeavors. If logically you think something might be good, but instinctively you're apprehensive—DON'T do it. Your mind and emotions must be in sync for success to occur.

❏ In the Surrounding Influences position, orange indicates that a balanced approach is affecting the matter at hand. Take it as a good sign.

❏ As an Obstacle, orange denotes that there is an imbalance. Be sure the situation is what you want.

❏ In the Past position, orange shows that a balanced, harmonious situation was attained.

❏ Orange in the Present position suggests that balance has been achieved, and now is the time to move on the matter.

❏ As an Outcome or in a Future position, orange signifies that a favorable, harmonious condition will be achieved if you continue on your course.

SPIRITUAL

Your approach to life is far more practical than that of the blind follower. There's an understanding and a balance to your thinking. You neither overemphasize nor de-emphasize your spiritual quest. Every experience is carefully weighed, then acted upon.

❑ As a Surrounding Influence, orange indicates that a practical approach to esoteric matters affects your attitude toward life. You've reached a balance within yourself.

❑ In the Obstacle position, orange suggests you need to stop balancing everything. It's time to accept some things on faith, or to develop a deeper understanding that some things cannot always be readily verified.

❑ In the Past position, orange shows that a practical approach to mystical or metaphysical matters was taken.

❑ In the Present position, orange indicates that you are carefully weighing matters of the spirit or higher awareness. Once you've weighed the matter, you will act according to what you sense is right.

❑ Orange as an Outcome or in a Future position reveals that the path you are following regarding spiritual matters will lead to harmony.

ORANGE (Intensified)

COLOR KEYS: Imbalance or overbalance. Irrational thought. Overemotional or overly logical.

EMOTIONAL

When you try to force matters to come out the way you want them, you're counteracting the natural balance of the elements. Consequently, you feel out of sync, or at odds with yourself. For example, you may be trying too hard to find the meaning of a relationship, or to make a love relationship out of one that isn't there. You could be distorting a friendship. The oracle suggests simply accepting the relationship for what it is.

❑ Intensified orange as a Surrounding Influence suggests that you are overbalancing, dealing with things too emotionally or too logically. You're going to extremes.

❑ If the color appears as an Obstacle, it indicates your emotions are out of balance, and that's the problem.

❑ In the Past position, intensified orange denotes that you've been performing a juggling act between your emotions and your logical mind, never quite reaching a balance.

❑ In the Present position, intensified orange signifies a nebulous situation, one in which there is an imbalance.

❑ As an Outcome or in a Future position, the color reveals that unless you take control of matters, you're headed toward an imbalance. The oracle suggests that it's up to you to balance emotions and logic.

MATERIAL

You're putting the wrong emphasis on your desires—confusing what you think you want with what you really want. The oracle suggests that now is the time to balance this out. You may be entering a career, business venture, or investment for all the wrong reasons.

☐ If intensified orange appears as a Surrounding Influence, it suggests that things around you are out of balance.

☐ In the Obstacle position, the color indicates that the goal you are trying to achieve is being blocked by an imbalance. More thought must be put into the situation.

☐ In the Past position, intensified orange shows that you behaved as though you were on a seesaw. You wavered between your emotions and your logic and allowed this confusion to get in the way.

☐ In the Present position, your emotions and your intellect are vying for control at this moment. Go back to step one for a clearer view of what you want. Then take it from there.

☐ As an Outcome or a Future position, you are headed toward an imbalance. Caution is advised. Look at the situation again. There is an adjustment needed.

SPIRITUAL

You are overbalancing—either taking things on faith too blindly and following paths leading nowhere, or you are overintellectualizing and building barriers that block your quest. An open heart and mind leads to the end of the rainbow.

☐ If intensified orange appears as a Surrounding Influence, everything around you is being distorted by your lack of balance. You're not accepting things as they are—only as you want to see them.

❑ As an Obstacle, intensified orange indicates that as long as your views are out of balance, you'll lack the order necessary to pursue your spiritual quest.

❑ In the Past position, your thinking did not reach a level of higher awareness because you were overbalancing.

❑ In the Present position, the color signifies that you must carefully weigh all aspects of your spiritual search. There is no balance.

❑ As an Outcome or in a Future position, intensified orange reveals that unless changes are made in your thinking and understanding, the path you are following will lead to confusion.

YELLOW

COLOR KEYS: Learning. Intellect. Logic. Legal documents. Order.

EMOTIONAL

You look on the bright side of things, but you tend to put your emotions aside for clarity. You react in a levelheaded manner and take a practical approach to your emotions. You do everything right, but not from an emotional basis. You keep everything very logical and scientific. You tend to act from what you have learned, rather than react to what you feel.

❑ Yellow in the Surrounding Influences position signifies you are in a learning situation. All the facts are in front of you. It's up to you to place them in their proper order.

❑ If yellow appears as an Obstacle, the indication is that you're reacting with your mind, not your heart. Put more emotion into the matter at hand.

❑ In the Past position, yellow shows that you already learned a lesson regarding the matter under consideration.

❑ In the Present position, yellow denotes that everything is in the proper order. With patience and a sensitivity toward your feelings, you can determine the outcome. Positive thinking is the pathway to harmony.

❑ As an Outcome or in a Future position, yellow suggests that the natural order is coming into place. Be confident. The future looks bright.

MATERIAL

Success obtained in this situation will usually come through the intellect. Legal papers or contracts are usually surrounding the person when this color appears. If there is an option for a contract or an extension of one, now is the time to put everything in order. This is the perfect time to buy, sell, or look for a promotion.

❑ If yellow appears as a Surrounding Influence, now is the time to move, to seek the change, present your plans, make your request. If more education is indicated, accept it.

❑ If yellow falls in the Obstacle position, your intellectual prowess may be intimidating others. A more personable approach is suggested.

❑ In the Past position, yellow shows that there was advancement regarding the matter at hand.

❑ In the Present position, yellow reveals the options are in front of you—education, a promotion, a contract, or other advances.

❑ With yellow as an Outcome or in a Future position, the outlook is bright—there's clear sailing ahead. Everything is falling into logical order. Rewards for clear and positive thinking will result.

SPIRITUAL

Your approach to a philosophy of life is clear and logical. You have put your thinking in order and have learned how to express yourself. You are both a fine teacher and an avid learner.

❏ Yellow as a Surrounding Influence suggests that you must select the philosophy of life or spiritual path that suits you best.

❏ If yellow appears as an Obstacle, the indication is that the matter under question must be put in order. Clear thinking is called for regarding matters of higher awareness or a spiritual quest.

❏ In the Past position, yellow indicates that you've spent time learning a philosophy or spiritual teaching.

❏ If yellow turns up in the Present position, the oracle suggests you remember that although you are the teacher, you are also the student. Take advantage of the fact that as you learn, you are also ordering your thoughts. By keeping an open and positive mind, you can draw on your knowledge and develop a philosophy that works best for you.

❏ If yellow appears in the Outcome or in a Future position, it indicates that the higher awareness you seek will be yours. It's up to you to absorb this new outlook and place it all in order.

YELLOW (Intensified)

COLOR KEYS: Illogical. Illegal activities. Intellectual blocks. Skeptical or cynical attitudes.

EMOTIONAL

Sometimes you become illogical when there is no set pattern before you. In such a situation, you need to trust your feelings rather than cold logic. Too much logic becomes illogical, especially in emotional matters.

In relationships, your tendency is not to bend. You are the dictator in any relationship. You want everything to follow a certain pattern. If it doesn't go that way, you move on to the next person. The oracle points out that intellect and logic are rarely key factors in relationships. Emotions are the important thing. A person who may be your logical choice may nevertheless be lacking in areas you're not considering.

❑ Intensified yellow as a Surrounding Influence suggests that illogical thoughts or actions are affecting your feelings. A dose of reason is needed.

❑ In the Obstacle position, intensified yellow shows that there is no logical approach to the emotions. As long as you choose to deal with your concern in such a manner, you won't find what you seek.

❑ In the Past position, the color indicates that you overanalyzed and overcategorized emotional matters. What did it get you?

❑ In the Present position, the color implies that if you don't get in touch with your emotions, you will find yourself alone with your logic.

❑ With intensified yellow as an Outcome or in a Future position, the indication is that you're looking for perfection. You may be in for a letdown unless you allow for flexibility in your thinking.

MATERIAL

Your thinking has become distorted by rigid and illogical thought. If your question concerns a business venture, this is not the time to buy or sell. In careers, don't look for an advancement or make any move at this time. If you are required to sign a contract, make sure you read the fine print.

❑ As a Surrounding Influence, intensified yellow indicates that you are being swayed or prompted in a direction that needs more consideration. It may lack order.

❑ As an Obstacle, intensified yellow indicates that illogical choices cloud your thinking. Be careful of legal traps and involvements.

❑ If intensified yellow falls in the Past, it shows that your thinking was distorted and in need of revision.

❑ With intensified yellow in the Present, your thinking is illogical and clouded by what you think you want rather than what really is. Learn to be more flexible in your thinking.

❑ As an Outcome or in a Future position, intensified yellow reveals that the direction you are heading in appears to be illogical. The oracle suggests revising and editing your thoughts into a more positive orientation. Otherwise, expect difficulties in achieving your goals.

SPIRITUAL

Intensified yellow is the color of the skeptic. You are

resistant to anything that isn't scientific, and are ruled by logic. The scientific aspects of your thinking act as a barrier to your search. Everything must be proven. You reduce philosophy to logical explanations even where logic does not apply.

❏ If intensified yellow appears as a Surrounding Influence, it signifies that in looking for order you have become enmeshed in your logical thinking to such a point in your search for higher awareness that you have become illogical.

❏ As an Obstacle, intensified yellow indicates that your logical thinking about spiritual matters has led you to illogical conclusions.

❏ In the Past position, your thinking about spiritual matters has been distorted and rigid. It needs an overhaul.

❏ In the Present position, intensified yellow indicates that rigid thinking with an overemphasis on logic presents barriers to spiritual growth. Go back over what you've learned and sort out the things that have confused you.

❏ As an Outcome or in a Future position, intensified yellow suggests that spiritual matters will seem illogical. Unless you allow more flexibility in your thoughts about what is possible, you'll be blocked by your own thinking.

GREEN

COLOR KEYS: Change. Growth. Healing. Money. Renewal. Birth. New ideas.

EMOTIONAL

You are open to changes in your life, someone who is looking ahead, wanting to grow. Self-improvement is a keen interest.

Regarding relationships, you may be meeting someone new, or revitalizing an old relationship. If you're in a relationship that is stagnant, or otherwise not meeting your needs, the oracle is suggesting a fresh start. Maybe you need to talk things over, come to a consensus on a matter that has been stewing for too long.

❑ When green turns up in the Surrounding Influences position, it suggests the desire for emotional growth. Possibly the matter you are asking about is starting a new relationship or revitalizing an existing one.

❑ In the Obstacles position, the oracle may be telling you that changes taking place in your life are posing problems. It may also be suggesting that you are afraid of making changes.

❑ In the Past position, green indicates there have been many changes, and you've been trying to adjust to them. One of these changes might have been a new relationship, or a new start.

❑ In the Present position, green signifies a fresh start or new beginnings regarding the matter at hand. Growth is indicated.

❑ If green appears as an Outcome or in a Future position, the outlook is for emotional growth or change. Matters will not stay where they are. You may revitalize an old relationship or meet someone new.

MATERIAL

An advancement or change in your career may be impending. There may be a modest raise or financial gain in the offing. Concerning business matters, the time is ripe for putting a new idea into motion, or expanding an existing one. Regarding finances, money is coming, but not necessarily a large sum.

❑ As a Surrounding Influence, green suggests that you've had a change of mind regarding your plans. It may seem that everything around you is changing. Growth is indicated.

❑ When green comes up as an Obstacle, it indicates that you are fighting change. Your energy is fighting against the changes that are needed.

❑ In the Past position, green shows that you have already made changes. A small financial increase could have resulted, or there may have been new beginnings with career or business matters.

❑ In the Present position, the color denotes a change of some sort is taking place. Don't worry about it. It's for the better.

❑ In the Outcome or in a Future position, green signifies that you should expect an advancement or growth in a matter at hand. If your question concerns starting a new business or a fresh start, the signs are favorable.

SPIRITUAL

Growth, expansion, and renewal are indicated in your spiritual quest or concern. Since green is the color of healing, it could indicate the beginning of a personal transformation. You may be questioning old beliefs, which now seem stale or outdated. Don't be afraid of change.

❑ As a Surrounding Influence, green suggests that matters in your life are prompting you to turn to spiritual concerns. Expansion of consciousness is at hand. You are wrapped in the excitement of new ideas and new thoughts, as well as the abilities that you are finding you possess.

❑ If green appears as an Obstacle, it implies that you may be fighting inner urges to grow or to renew yourself. While you may be outwardly content with material success, twinges of unease may indicate that your inner self or unconscious is pushing you to explore the spiritual realms to fulfill needs that have remained dormant. If you fight those urges, you may find less and less satisfaction with your material gain.

❑ Green in the Past position shows that your awareness has grown from past experience.

❑ If green is rolled in the Present position, it indicates that you're reevaluating your ideas and are on the path of growth. For example, if you have neither believed nor disbelieved in life after death, you may be presently examining or seeking evidence that life exists beyond the physical body.

❑ As an Outcome or in a Future position, green denotes that change brings growth and acceptance of new ideas and new thoughts. In the Future position, green hints of a new world opening in your spiritual quest. Expect enlightenment and understanding in what you seek. As you grow, the barriers around you will dissolve. You might consider delving into the healing arts. You may have abilities you haven't tapped.

GREEN (Intensified)

COLOR KEYS: Deceit. Treachery. Duplicity. Camouflage. Envy. Unnecessary change.

EMOTIONAL

You're always on the path of change, never stopping to smell the flowers or to allow any relationships to blossom. There's no stability; you're an emotional chameleon. Instead of sharing, you're competing. Jealousy is your green-eyed monster.

❑ As a Surrounding Influence, intensified green requires you to ask yourself what it is you really want. You're saying "yes," but inside you may not feel it's worth it.

❑ As an Obstacle, intensified green suggests that impatience and envy are your barriers. You must put aside your petty concerns and focus on the positive aspects of life.

❑ In the Past position, intensified green shows that although there were changes, you were not happy with any you made.

❑ In the Present position, the color signifies you may be overreacting to circumstances around you as a result of your own insecurity. You need to reevaluate a matter or make positive changes that will lead to what you seek.

❑ As an Outcome or in a Future position, intensified green means you shouldn't force change. You may be dissatisfied with the results if you do. The oracle warns that you should avoid taking action out of fear or insecurity.

MATERIAL

You're bouncing around too much. You're being side-tracked, making too many changes. Trying to take too many paths usually leads to blind alleys. Regarding finances, you may feel you're on the right path, but be careful not to scatter your energies.

❏ If intensified green appears as a Surrounding Influence, indications are that all the changes taking place around you are not for the better. The oracle suggests that you consider sticking with what you know.

❏ In the Obstacle position, the color signifies that you are too scattered. Attempting to make changes now could mean trouble.

❏ In the Past position, intensified green shows that changes led to deceit or duplicity. They weren't what they appeared or were supposed to be.

❏ Intensified green in the Present position reveals that you are making unnecessary or unwarranted changes. They're being made for the wrong reasons. Positive thinking is required.

❏ As an Outcome position or in a Future position, intensified green implies that the path of change you are on leads to blind alleys. The results will be instability unless action to modify the changes is taken.

SPIRITUAL

You may be deceiving yourself as to what is necessary and what is not necessary for your growth and development. Because a philosophy works for someone else doesn't mean it's going to work for you. You may not have the same abilities or talents, so stop camouflaging the truth. Each of us must develop at our own pace, and according to our own abilities.

Because it takes one person longer than another doesn't mean he or she is on the wrong path.

❑ If intensified green appears as a Surrounding Influence on a question regarding your spiritual path, the indication is that the environment surrounding your quest may be tainted by deceit and treachery. Something may appear as one thing, but be something else altogether.

❑ As an Obstacle, intensified green reveals that the tactics you are using may not allow you to achieve your goals. Closely consider your true feelings. If they don't match the image you're projecting, something must change.

❑ Appearing in the Past position, intensified green suggests that you deceived yourself in the past. The green light said "go," but in the intensified tone it indicated you were not prepared to achieve what you had in mind.

❑ When intensified green appears in the Present, the color signifies you may be wearing someone else's cloak. You like the fabric and the style, but it's not yours. You may be acting like the person who makes a show of reverence or piety, but whose actual thoughts and actions are something else altogether. The indication is that you need to reevaluate your present beliefs. Make sure the path you follow is your own.

❑ As an Outcome or in the Future positions, intensified green serves as a warning. If you're mimicking others you envy, or camouflaging what you truly feel, then spiritual growth, healing, rebirth, or transformation are not the likely result.

BLUE

COLOR KEYS: Serenity. Tranquility. Sensitivity. Devotion. Introverted. Private.

EMOTIONAL

You alternately feel a sense of tranquility and a desire for solitude. While your sensitivity may be hidden, it is nonetheless real. Even though you may act the part of the macho man or the carefree woman, your act is a way of protecting your feelings. You may be a devoted partner in an emotionally intense relationship, but outwardly you don't show it.

❑ If you roll blue as a Surrounding Influence, the indication is that everything is tranquil concerning the matter at hand. At this moment there is a sense of calm and tranquility.

❑ As an Obstacle, blue indicates you're keeping your feelings inside. You may not be willing to give up your peace of mind to seek a new relationship or to make any sort of emotional change. You're being lulled by your own feelings of tranquility into accepting whatever is around you.

❑ In the Past position, blue shows that everything was quiet and peaceful around you.

❑ In the Present position, the color signifies that you've achieved your peace of mind in the matter at hand. Your feelings are protected.

❑ If blue appears as an Outcome or in a Future position, it suggests that you may soon be entering a period of tranquility.

MATERIAL

The situation does not call for change. There are too many inhibitions. This is a time in which you should count your blessings, and hold your peace. Regarding careers, the oracle suggests that the time is not right for seeking either a raise or a promotion.

❑ As a Surrounding Influence, blue indicates that there is no change. Things are calm and peaceful surrounding you.

❑ As an Obstacle, the color reveals that you are being too complacent. You're lulled by a false sense of security.

❑ If blue appears in the Past, there was no energy put forth in the matter. Everything stayed status quo.

❑ In the Present position, blue signifies that the matter at hand is falling into order. Everything is moving along quietly. Call on your internal voice to guide you.

❑ As an Outcome or in a Future position, blue reveals that if you are looking for peace of mind you will achieve it. However, most of what you'll accomplish will depend on your own thoughts and actions. Seek guidance from within.

SPIRITUAL

The inner peace you achieve is satisfying to your soul. You go within and seek solitude. You are devoted and loyal to your beliefs. Introspection is a key word here.

❑ If your concern is related to spiritual endeavors, and blue appears as a Surrounding Influence, the path that you're following leads to tranquility. In essence, you are engulfing yourself in the blue depths of the cosmic sea.

❏ In the Obstacle position, blue indicates that although you achieve peace of mind, it is also a solitary and sometimes lonely path.

❏ In the Past position, the color shows that you were seeking tranquility and solitude. You may have separated yourself from situations involving conflict.

❏ In the Present position, blue indicates that your path has led to tranquility and peace of mind.

❏ As an Outcome or in a Future position, blue reveals that the probable outlook is for your spiritual devotion to lead to inner peace.

BLUE (Intensified)

COLOR KEYS: Isolation. Loneliness. Depression.

EMOTIONAL

With intensified blue, the situation is more solitary than with the lighter hue. You may be withholding things from your partner, which is causing concern. Your emotional state could lead you into a deep blue funk.

❏ If intensified blue turns up as a Surrounding Influence, the indication is that you're being affected by an isolated situation. You're set apart from others.

❏ As an Obstacle, intensified blue implies that by holding back all you feel and isolating yourself from people and situations, you're not allowing yourself to achieve what you are seeking.

❏ In the Past position, the color signifies that you felt isolated and alone, possibly alienated from a particular person.

❏ In the Present position, intensified blue suggests a solitary situation. If this doesn't suit you, the oracle suggests that you change it.

❏ As an Outcome or a Future position, intensified blue reveals that unless there is a radical change, circumstances will isolate you, increasing your loneliness and solitude.

MATERIAL

In the Material category, intensified blue suggests an inability to express oneself. A negative attitude is inhibiting your abilities. You are internalizing everything. The oracle suggests that you create a more positive atmosphere around yourself, and open up to others. In financial matters, there is no viable basis for monetary gain. The oracle suggests that you confer with others, then choose your direction.

❑ As a Surrounding Influence, intensified blue indicates that you're being isolated by circumstances. You may feel as though you are in limbo, but try to maintain a positive outlook in spite of everything.

❑ If intensified blue appears as an Obstacle, the oracle is suggesting that you are too self-centered. If your concern is your job or career, the only thing wrong with it is yourself and your inhibitions. Focus on an aspect of the job that you find positive and use that as a basis for changing your view of it. This advice can be used in any material matter under inquiry.

❑ In the Past position, the color signifies that you found yourself isolated. While you stayed stuck on your "desert island," you could never get ahead. You may have found yourself depressed and bored with your situation.

❑ In the Present position, intensified blue reveals that the matter of concern is being internalized. You are not expressing yourself. You're forgetting that others can help you. In the material world, you need other people. You can't stand alone. Open up to suggestions offered by others. You've allowed yourself to become too solitary.

❑ As an Outcome or in a Future position, intensified blue is a warning that the outcome could be bleak. Unless you make a radical change in your thinking, you could find yourself isolated. The oracle encourages positive thinking. If you can find one glimmer of light, you can find the whole rainbow.

SPIRITUAL

Introspection and isolation do not necessarily enhance personal growth. In this case, they only lead to more inhibitions. In order to reach a level of understanding, you must open up and experience life. Spiritual growth is meant to be shared, not isolated. Be careful about what you decide to devote yourself to. Don't get lost in your search by making it too internalized.

❏ Intensified blue as a Surrounding Influence indicates that your spiritual quest is too isolated, which only inhibits your growth.

❏ In the Obstacle position, the color suggests you are too solitary in your seeking. You need to accept views from other people. The more barriers you create around you, the more difficult it is for others to reach you.

❏ If intensified blue appears in the Past position, it means you were isolated in your search. You lacked the support and encouragement others could provide.

❏ In the Present position, intensified blue signifies that you are following a solitary path in your search for higher awareness. Closely consider the reason for this situation. If you are avoiding others because their ideas might conflict with your own, you may be avoiding growth.

❏ As an Outcome or in a Future position, the color implies that you are on a course leading to spiritual isolation. Don't allow yourself to become too self-absorbed or isolated. Changes now could avoid an unwanted outcome.

PURPLE

COLOR KEYS: Rules and regulations. Tradition. The past. The romantic.

EMOTIONAL

You are the romantic living in the past. You control your emotions with rules and regulations. You're not the type who would allow your passions to run wild, unless they dealt with something or someone from the past. You don't accept new things quickly or easily, and sometimes place limitations on yourself.

Regarding relationships, you need order. Until you have it, you can't relax. If you're seeking a new relationship, consider looking for one element that is familiar. For example, someone new might remind you of a person from the past, or a place where you meet might resemble a place you know from your past. The comparison will be comforting.

❏ As a Surrounding Influence, purple denotes many rules and regulations affecting you. Make sure you're fully aware of them.

❏ If purple appears as an Obstacle, you're allowing the past to stop you from moving ahead. You may be regulating your emotions, adding rules that may not be necessary. You allow the past to blind you to opportunities for new starts.

❏ In the Past position, the indication is that rules and regulations were restrictive. The matter of concern did not progress beyond these limits.

❏ With purple in the Present position, the color signifies you have found order and structure in your life, and are dealing with what is familiar. Through past experience, you've learned to find the right direction.

❑ As an Outcome and in a Future position, the outlook is that you'll have to deal with rules and regulations, and with what is familiar. If you must repeat the past, deal with it wisely.

MATERIAL

There can be material success if you deal with what you're familiar with. You plod along with things that you know, but you tend not to be innovative or to take chances. You're comfortable with rules and regulations. You fit in well, but leave leadership to others.

❑ Purple as a Surrounding Influence suggests that shades of the past surround you. You must dig deep within for the help you need in choosing your direction. This is not a new situation in which you find yourself. You must decide how to deal with the rules and regulations.

❑ As an Obstacle, the color denotes that you may be letting rules and regulations bind you. Don't repeat past mistakes. The rules and regulations can be changed by taking a different approach.

❑ In the Past position, purple indicates that you dealt with structures of rules and regulations, leaving few openings for anything new. You may have felt that you'd fallen into a rut.

❑ If purple appears in the Present position, the oracle advises dealing only with what you find familiar. For example, stay with stocks with a proven track record, or follow a career advancement that allows you to remain in your specialization.

❑ When purple appears as an Outcome or in a Future position, look to your past and consider the changes you've previously made. If you haven't fared well, be cautious about what's ahead. If you can structure your future based on past experience, you'll have better luck dealing with it.

SPIRITUAL

You are loyal and devoted, but in need of a philosophy that has rules and regulations to follow. Your beliefs are conditioned by past experiences.

❏ If you are thinking about the path your life is following and purple appears as a Surrounding Influence, the indication is that a system of beliefs is playing a strong role in your spiritual search. Be careful not to restrict your thinking to only what you know.

❏ As an Obstacle, purple suggests that you take a close look at what you're being told to believe. Make sure it is in line with your own thoughts about life. If not, the rules and regulations of the belief system might be blocking your spiritual advancement.

❏ Purple in the Past suggests that religious structure has been very important to you, although it may be an unconscious rather than a conscious awareness. Your life has been structured to believe in whatever you've been taught as true.

❏ In the Present position, purple means that you are guided by the past. Everything that is going on right now is reminiscent of the past. Beware of falling into a spiritual rut.

❏ As an Outcome or in a Future position, the outlook is that you'll be bound by rules and regulations or by tradition in any spiritual quest. Structure and order is paramount in your life.

PURPLE (Intensified)

COLOR KEYS: Restrictions. Narrow-minded thinking. Rigidly tied to the past.

EMOTIONAL

The deeper shade of purple intensifies the ideas conveyed by the lighter hue, increasing the limitations and restrictions. You rarely forget a slight or a hurt—anything done to you. You can be vindictive. A habit once learned is very hard for you to discard. You are bound by your own belief system, rarely opening up to new experiences.

Regarding a relationship, you may want it for all the wrong reasons—security and remembrances of the past are not enough now. If there is no free flow of thought and feelings, the situation could be stifling for one or both of you.

❏ If intensified purple appears as a Surrounding Influence, it signifies that you are being affected by matters of the past, and making the same mistakes over and over.

❏ As an Obstacle, the color denotes that you are bound by numerous restrictions. The oracle suggests you learn to bend.

❏ In the Past position, intensified purple shows that severe restrictions abounded, stifling emotional growth. You've been on an emotional merry-go-round going in circles, never reaching anywhere new.

❏ In the Present position, intensified purple suggests you may be crippled by rules and regulations, by the many restrictions placed upon you.

❏ As an Outcome or in a Future position, intensified

purple indicates that you'll be bogged down by your limitations and restrictions. The obstacles that you faced in the past will loom before you once more. The oracle suggests a drastic change of thoughts and ideas is needed to avoid repeating the past. Build on the aspects of your life that make you happy. Avoid putting energy into the aspects that have caused problems in the past.

MATERIAL

Your ties with the past are holding you down. You may be relying too heavily on past achievements. Regarding a career, you need to set new goals. Consider the possibility of breaking with old ways in order to recover lost ground.

❏ If intensified purple appears as a Surrounding Influence, it reveals that past circumstances that were oppressive are influencing matters at hand. Make sure you're not simply repeating the past. The oracle suggests you carefully consider the option of striking out in a new direction free from past influences.

❏ As an Obstacle, intensified purple indicates that you are making the same mistakes you made in the past. Instead of opening new doors, you are building barriers around you.

❏ In the Past position, the color signifies that the matter of concern was oppressive. Too many rules and regulations restricted your thinking.

❏ In the Present position, intensified purple denotes that the rules and regulations you've set for yourself reign supreme. They don't leave any room for progress.

❏ As an Outcome or in a Future position, intensified purple suggests that overly cautious behavior could limit or

restrict you. You need to adjust your thinking to a more positive path.

SPIRITUAL

You may not realize the rigidity of the structure of your
past religious training. Adhering to a traditional philosophy
just because you were born into it may be creating barriers to
new ideas, broader horizons. Your devotion may be by habit,
not choice.

❑ As a Surrounding Influence, intensified purple indicates that your spiritual path is heavily influenced by self-
deception. Clear your thinking. You may want to seek a new
path free of the old.

❑ As an Obstacle, intensified purple is telling you that
the restrictions you've placed on yourself are not the way to
enlightenment.

❑ In the Past position, the color shows that you were
heavily influenced by rigid ideas or beliefs. The first step toward change is the realization that these beliefs have retarded
your search.

❑ In the Present position, intensified purple denotes
that you cling to the past. You're not allowing yourself to
break away from the old programming, which may be inhibiting your growth.

❑ As an Outcome or in a Future position, the color
warns that the path you are following could lead to more
restrictions and limitations, and ultimately to self-deception.

PINK

COLOR KEYS: Tenderness. Gentle love. Sensitivity. Vitality. Maintenance of health.

EMOTIONAL

You are a true romantic, guided by love in its most unblemished form. This is lasting love. Pink also speaks of the adage: A healthy mind in a healthy body. Your emotional health is promoted by love of self. The body is the temple of the mind to which you pay homage by keeping fit. Regarding relationships, love is all that counts.

❏ Pink as a Surrounding Influence suggests that love or a health matter is affecting your concern.

❏ As an Obstacle, pink suggests that matters of the heart are blocking you from achieving your goal. Come to terms with the situation. You may have to make a decision.

❏ If pink appears in the Past position, the color shows that love or a health matter may have affected your concern.

❏ In the Present situation, the indication is that everything is in the pink. Regarding love and romance or a health question, matters couldn't be better.

❏ As an Outcome or a Future position, pink indicates a bright outlook. Vitality and energy will be present. In relationships, it would lead to love.

MATERIAL

Approach the material with your natural vitality, self-confidence, and great sensitivity and you are assured of success. If a career or business situation is being contemplated, rely on your positive thinking to build your self-confidence. You are the master of all you pursue.

❏ As a Surrounding Influence, pink indicates the matter at hand is being affected positively. The situation is healthy.

❏ As an Obstacle, pink indicates that your optimistic views may be blinding you to reality. Take a closer look at all the factors involved.

❏ In the Past position, pink indicates that the situation has been healthy. You've been on the right track.

❏ In the Present position, the color suggests that the matter under question is healthy and positive.

❏ If pink appears as an Outcome or in a Future position, the outlook is healthy. Continue on your course.

SPIRITUAL

Love prompts you to be a more positive thinker. Your unselfish approach to life and your love of humanity make you aware of your higher self. Your beliefs and the love and energy you put into them revitalize you. Your spiritual slogan is: God is love.

❏ Pink as a Surrounding Influence suggests that your spiritual search is being affected positively by the love that you put forth in all you do.

❏ If you roll pink in the Obstacle position, the inference is that you are being blinded by your own feelings of love. You overlook the negative—the traps one can fall into.

❏ In the Past position, pink shows that your love of life has played a role in matters of high consciousness.

❑ In the Present position, pink indicates that you glow with love and vitality. You are on the right spiritual path. The love you are seeking is available to you.

❑ As an Outcome, or in a Future position, pink denotes that you will grow spiritually from your ability to love.

PINK (Intensified)

COLOR KEYS: Loss of vitality. Lack of love. Concern with health. Self-love.

EMOTIONAL

You are in love with the idea of being in love, but presently feeling the lack of love. A loss of vitality makes you think rather meditatively. In relationships, you hunger for love, but yet you love only yourself.

❑ As a Surrounding Influence, intensified pink suggests that you're being sapped by concerns about health or love.

❑ As an Obstacle, a loss of vitality or lack of love is blocking you from achieving what you've set out to accomplish.

❑ In the Past position, intensified pink reveals that a lack of love or poor health played a role in the matter at hand.

❑ In the Present position, intensified pink indicates your situation is not a healthy one.

❑ As an Outcome or in a Future position, intensified pink leads to a lack of love, or lack of vitality. The oracle suggests you change your thinking. Become less self-centered. Use your energy in a more positive way.

MATERIAL

A lack of vitality threatens to ruin your plans. You must think positively and work to improve your physical well-being, or you may not reach your material goals, whatever they may be.

❏ As a Surrounding Influence, intensified pink suggests that your lack of vitality and negative thinking have affected the matter at hand. There may be a health problem.

❏ As an Obstacle, the indication is that your lack of enthusiasm or your need for self-gratification act as barriers to your goals.

❏ In the Past position, intensified pink reveals that a lack of vitality or a love concern hindered you.

❏ In the Present position, the color indicates that unless you put more enthusiasm into what you do, you stand to lose whatever progress you've made.

❏ In the Outcome or a Future position, intensified pink implies that your path is cluttered by obstacles you've set up by your own self-centered thinking. The oracle reminds you that if you don't like the outlook, take the time and energy to change it by action.

SPIRITUAL

The line between self-love and selfless love is very thin. An imbalance can create spiritual malaise or blindness. You must achieve a balance between the logical and the emotional aspects of any philosophy.

❏ Intensified pink as a Surrounding Influence suggests that a preoccupation with self-aggrandizement is affecting your spiritual quest.

❏ In the Obstacle position, the color indicates that an obsessive concern with self is interfering with your spiritual search. The oracle suggests that you step aside from preoccupation with the self and into universal consciousness.

❏ In the Past position, intensified pink indicates that

your inflated ego led you astray, making you blind to the higher order of things.

❑ In the Present position, unless you put aside your preoccupation with the self, the path you follow will be a difficult one.

❑ As an Outcome or in a Future position, intensified pink warns that an inflated ego is leading you astray on your quest.

BROWN

COLOR KEYS: Solid foundations. Security. Stability.
A fertile time.

EMOTIONAL

You have your feet on the ground. You are stable, secure, down to Earth. You're in touch with your emotions. In relationships, you are the "salt of the Earth." You look for security, a solid foundation. The home is very important.

❑ If you roll brown as a Surrounding Influence, the indication is that stable influences are affecting you. They are prompting you to feel more secure.

❑ Brown as an Obstacle denotes that you may be seeking security prematurely. Sometimes seeds take time to grow.

❑ If brown appears in the Past, the color shows that you have set your foundations for emotional security, or planted seeds. The color that follows will tell how the seeds have grown.

❑ In the Present position, brown signifies that now is a fertile time for emotional security to take root. You are more secure and happy now than you've been for a while.

❑ As an Outcome or in the near Future position, brown implies that a sound emotional foundation is forming and will be realized.

MATERIAL

Brown is the essence of the material realm. The basis for success is firm. You are sure of achieving all that you set out to do. Expect stability if you don't already have it. If you do, you will build on it and multiply your assets.

❏ As a Surrounding Influence, brown indicates that you are being heavily affected by what is firm and stable. You will reap benefits from it.

❏ As an Obstacle, the oracle suggests that you are looking only at the material, and ignoring other important aspects that may be present.

❏ In the Past position, brown reveals that a firm foundation was laid at an earlier time. There was security, possibly a generous monetary award.

❏ In the Present position, brown signifies that you've attained security and stability. If the concern was money, it's no longer a problem.

❏ As an Outcome or in a Future position, the color portends positive results. You can expect to achieve whatever you are seeking, and don't be surprised if the benefits are greater than you expected.

SPIRITUAL

You put your higher consciousness to use in your everyday activities. You are able to function and make use of it in all your endeavors. You may think of it as positive thinking or creative visualization.

❏ As a Surrounding Influence, brown suggests that your spiritual quest is being swayed by practical considerations.

❏ As an Obstacle, brown hints that you are sometimes too practical in your approach to the spiritual realms. You need to go out on a limb once in a while.

❑ In the Past position, brown signifies that your spiritual quest has been a stable influence.

❑ In the Present position, the indication is that your search is well anchored. You put your knowledge of higher things to work for you.

❑ If brown appears as an Outcome or in a Future position, the color denotes that you will remain well rooted in any spiritual undertaking. You're not the type to get lost in the clouds.

BROWN (Intensified)

COLOR KEYS: Excessive materialism. Instability. Insecurity.

EMOTIONAL

You are too insecure. You lack confidence, and stability. Your emotions are too raw. In relationships, you may be overly blunt. Your insecurity may damage relationships. You may think more about money than people. You have a tendency to be self-centered.

❏ If intensified brown appears as the Surrounding Influence, it suggests that too much concern about stability and security are affecting the matter at hand. The oracle suggests more honesty and love are needed in the relationship.

❏ As an Obstacle, intensified brown suggests that your insecurities are blocking you from achieving what you are hoping to attain. Show more confidence, but avoid being self-centered.

❏ In the Past position, intensified brown shows that your feelings of insecurity affected the matter under question. Your concerns for stability were too strong and restricted growth.

❏ In the Present position, the color signifies that there is too much concern about the security of the matter at hand. Take things in stride. Worrying doesn't help.

❏ As an Outcome or in a Future position, the indication is that the path you are following will lead to intense concern about stability and security. It's your option to make the changes you need to avoid such an outcome.

MATERIAL

An obsessive preoccupation with material concerns hinders you from achieving what you desire. If you were considering expanding your business or making an investment, intensified brown in any position would indicate a negative outcome. Be careful you're not ruled by greed. It's better to stick to the tried and true at this time. Otherwise, you may overextend yourself.

❑ As a Surrounding Influence, intensified brown suggests that material concerns are weighing you down. These influences should be put in their proper place.

❑ In the Obstacle position, the color indicates an obsessive concern about finances, security, stability, or career that can block you from achieving success.

❑ In the Past position, intensified brown signifies that there has been too much preoccupation with material concerns.

❑ If the color appears in the Present position, the indication is that an obsession with material matters is controlling your life. Your aggressiveness, which you use to achieve your security, could work against you. You may alienate others around you.

❑ As an Outcome or in a Future position, intensified brown warns you to watch what seeds you plant because you have to live with the results. Unless you make some changes, you may find yourself overextended.

SPIRITUAL

Your thoughts and beliefs are bogged down by a preoccupation with the material. Thoughts and philosophies are muddied by your rigid, earthbound thinking.

❑ As a Surrounding Influence, intensified brown reveals that matters of higher consciousness are unduly affected by your set, earthbound thinking. Seek a balance.

❑ As an Obstacle, intensified brown indicates that your spiritual path is blocked by your obsessive testing of what is real. This concern is caused by your insecurity.

❑ In the Past position, the indication is that the desire for stability and material gain has overridden any interest in spiritual matters.

❑ In the Present position, intensified brown signifies that your own stubbornness is weighing you down in spiritual matters. Your overconcern with a practical and material approach won't lead to spiritual understanding.

❑ As an Outcome or in the Future position, intensified brown suggests that your search will be fettered by material concerns. Disillusionment is a likely result unless you can put material and emotional concerns in their rightful place.

PEACH

COLOR KEYS: Balance. Mellowness. Happiness.

EMOTIONAL

You've achieved an emotional balance. You're at peace with yourself. Regarding relationships, you have come to terms with the person you love. You are well suited for each other, and happy. If there is no other person in your life at this time, that's the way you want it.

❑ As a Surrounding Influence, peach suggests that everything around you is mellow. All indications are favorable.

❑ In the Obstacle position, the color implies you've become too complacent. Action is called for.

❑ In the Past position, peach signifies that you have learned to balance your emotions.

❑ In the Present position, the color shows that you are reaching a balance. You're at peace with yourself, and have come to terms with your emotions.

❑ As an Outcome or in a Future position, peach reveals that the road ahead is paved with happiness. You will achieve the balance you seek.

MATERIAL

Your financial outlook is bright. However, your happy-go-lucky nature makes you something of a spendthrift. The oracle warns you not to spend all your extra money on luxuries. Put some of it away.

Regarding a career question, things are going well, and

you should be happy about it. But keep your eyes open. Don't get overconfident. The situation could change.

❑ Peach as a Surrounding Influence indicates that everything around you is very positive. It's a good time for speculation, a good time for decisions. The aura around you is one of balance.

❑ If peach appears as an Obstacle, it means that you are looking at the world through rose-colored glasses, forgetting to stay in touch with reality.

❑ In the Past position, the color shows that you made wise, balanced decisions, and should have collected the fruits of your labor.

❑ In the Present position, peach implies that you have achieved happiness and balance. If you gauge success with happiness, you've achieved it.

❑ As an Outcome or in a Future position, the color signifies that by following the path you're on, you will achieve happiness and balance.

SPIRITUAL

You find joy through your search for higher meaning in life. You love the process of seeking—the end results aren't as important to you as the steps you take to get there. Preaching the word to others isn't that important to you. Your happiness in itself serves as an example that others can strive to attain.

❑ As a Surrounding Influence, peach indicates that a feeling of joy and contentment is prompting your spiritual search.

❑ As an Obstacle, peach shows that a spiritual awakening is being slowed or blocked by a sense of complacency caused by your mellowness and contentment.

❑ In the Past position, peach signifies that you achieved balance and peace in your spiritual quest.

❑ In the Present position, the color suggests that the spiritual doors are open. All you have to do is enter.

❑ As an Outcome or in a Future position, peach reveals that the path ahead leads to joy and contentment.

Remember, there is no intensified aspect of the color peach.

VIOLET

COLOR KEYS: The highest order of anything. Wisdom. Spirituality. Idealism. Love of Humanity.

EMOTIONAL

Your emotions are reflections of your spirituality. You offer love without stipulation. You are beyond petty emotional entreaties or pompous, sanctimonious appeals for attention. Love of self and selfless love are no contradiction for you. Your emotions are in harmony with the highest possible expression of love.

Regarding a romance, violet suggests that your partner could be a soulmate. It's a union of profound love.

❑ Violet as a Surrounding Influence suggests that you deal with emotional matters in a highly positive way. The influences are supportive.

❑ If violet appears as an Obstacle, it may mean that others are envious of all you have, and place blocks in your path. The oracle suggests: Remain content and patient and the barriers will crumble.

❑ Violet in the Past implies that emotionally you were or have been on a path of the highest order.

❑ In the Present position, violet indicates that you've attained the highest order of what you've set out to achieve. Any baser motives would not be fulfilling. It could retard your growth or expression. In the emotional sense, you've added the white light of understanding to the purple—the past and limitation—and now are aware of what has led you to your present situation.

❏ As an Outcome or in the Future positions, violet denotes that you will achieve the understanding that will balance you emotionally. You're on the right path, the path of completion.

MATERIAL

In the material realm, violet represents the highest order of things. Keep on your course, and be confident that whatever you need will come to you. You can expect to complete any matter that you're dealing with.

❏ If violet appears as a Surrounding Influence, the indication is that the highest order of whatever concerns you is playing a role.

❏ As an Obstacle, violet is a warning not to allow yourself to be bogged down by the trivial. Seek the highest aspect of whatever you are pursuing.

❏ In the Past position, violet signifies that your priorities dealt with understanding the highest order of matters.

❏ In the Present position, the color means that you are achieving the highest order of what you've set out to attain. You've been preparing for what is now happening.

❏ With violet as an Outcome and in a Future position, the outlook is for achievement of your highest goals. You have a universal outlook that is taking you above the average. You've learned that the abundance you seek lies within you, and that all you have to do is open yourself to it and it will be there.

SPIRITUAL

You rise above both the material and the emotional so

that everything you do is for the universal good. The humanist fits here. This is the spiritual path of high wisdom, expanded consciousness. You are the spiritual guide, and therefore a teacher.

❑ If violet appears as a Surrounding Influence, the indication is that the circumstances of your spiritual quest are of the highest order.

❑ In the Obstacle position, violet suggests that the goal of your quest is so high that it sometimes seems impossible to achieve. Keep a positive perspective, and know that the more difficult the challenge, the greater the reward.

❑ In the Past position, violet shows that you rose above the material and emotional and stepped onto the path of universal happiness.

❑ In the Present position, the color signifies that you have reached an elevated plateau of understanding. Spiritual fulfillment is at hand.

❑ As an Outcome or in a Future position, violet denotes that you are on the right path, exactly where you should be. The highest order of your search will be revealed.

There is no intensified violet.

GOLD

COLOR KEYS: Success. Creative thought. Attainment of goals. Positive thinking.

EMOTIONAL

A positive sense of being makes you happy and healthy. Regarding a relationship, all your desires will be fulfilled. It couldn't look better for you.

❏ As a Surrounding Influence, gold indicates that a positive environment is playing a role related to your emotional concern.

❏ As an Obstacle, gold suggests that the goals you set for yourself may be too high. Take one step at a time.

❏ In the Past position, the color denotes that your positive thoughts and feelings have been appreciated.

❏ In the Present position, gold shows that you are now attaining the emotional goals you've set out to achieve.

❏ As an Outcome or in a Future position, gold reveals that your desires will be fulfilled.

MATERIAL

Success is at your fingertips. You will reach all your goals related to finances, career, and material concerns. You have the Midas touch.

❏ As a Surrounding Influence, gold indicates that the factors around you are favorable. Now it's up to you to take action. This is the best position for gold.

❏ As an Obstacle, gold shows that you are a perfectionist. Your high standards may be out of your reach.

❑ In the Past position, gold signifies that you were heading for success. All the aspects were favorable. It should have been a time of money or awards.

❑ In the Present position, the color denotes that success is at hand. You are overcoming all that has blocked you.

❑ As an Outcome or in a Future position, gold reveals that all you are hoping for will be achieved.

SPIRITUAL

Your mind is geared for success. Your positive thinking opens doors. Whatever you are seeking is within reach. You can attain it.

❑ As a Surrounding Influence, gold suggests that a positive environment is working in your favor.

❑ If gold appears as an Obstacle, it denotes that an overabundance of success has made you view the spiritual search as lacking challenge. Without such a challenge, the objective seems less enticing.

❑ Gold in the Past position shows that you were on a successful spiritual path. Learn from what you were doing right.

❑ Gold in the Present reveals that your higher aspirations are now being achieved.

❑ As an Outcome or in a Future position, gold signifies that you are on the right path. By going forward with your quest, your goals will soon be within reach.

★ ★ ★

There is no intensified gold.

SILVER

COLOR KEYS: Versatility. Flexibility. Intuition. Psychic awareness.

EMOTIONAL

You are guided by your inner feelings and must learn to trust them. Look within, gauge your feelings, and measure the true essence of your thoughts.

In a relationship, you may be looking at what the relationship could be, rather than at what it is right now. The oracle suggests that you let your intuition be your guide. If it feels right, do it. If not, don't.

❑ As a Surrounding Influence, silver suggests that there is an intuitive awareness around you. Watch the signs. Stay flexible.

❑ As an Obstacle, silver indicates that you are being too nebulous, building castles in the air, while disregarding your own intuition. You should listen to your inner voice.

❑ With silver in the Past position, the indication is that previously you used your intuition when you needed it.

❑ If silver appears in the Present position, it signifies that all the answers you need are available to you. Simply look within.

❑ As an Outcome or in a Future position, silver reveals that the outcome is psychic insight. Once you learn to trust your feelings, you will grow emotionally.

MATERIAL

Your success could be measured by your own positive

thinking. The inner guidance you receive is usually accurate. However, the oracle gives this warning: Do not let wishful thinking color your thoughts. Proceed with care. The danger is that you may be advancing too rapidly and not paying enough attention to what is going on around you.

❑ As a Surrounding Influence, silver suggests that you take a close look at the circumstances around you. They may not be what they seem. Things may look one way but feel another. Let your intuition guide you.

❑ As an Obstacle, silver implies that wishful thinking rather than concrete action may be keeping you from achieving your goal.

❑ In the Past position, silver signifies that you followed your inner guidance on this matter. Look back to see what you learned from it.

❑ In the Present position, the indication is that you are allowing your intuition to guide you. Make sure you don't move too fast, even if everything feels right.

❑ As an Outcome or in a Future position, silver reveals that flexibility and insightful awareness may be the result.

SPIRITUAL

Silver is a color of psychic energy and is at home in the spiritual domain. However, this placement can have two meanings—either you are already in touch with the spiritual and can trust your thoughts and feelings, or you *need* to get in touch with your inner feelings.

❑ As a Surrounding Influence, silver indicates that the psychic energy that surrounds you will guide you.

❑ In the Obstacle position, silver signifies that you're

not trusting yourself. Don't follow a particular path just because that's what "everyone else" is doing. Seek the path that is best suited to you.

❏ In the Past position, the color shows that you were moving along your own path. Silver is closely aligned with individuality in thought as opposed to the group mind or the restrictive beliefs of a cult.

❏ In the Present position, silver signifies psychic awareness. Your inner self has guided you to search for a higher awareness.

❏ As an Outcome or in a Future position, silver means that your path is leading you toward insightfulness and understanding.

There is no intensified silver.

GREY

COLOR KEYS: Confusion and misunderstanding. Fear. Despondency.

EMOTIONAL

Despondency and confusion muddy your thoughts and feelings. Until the matter at hand is clear, very little can be resolved.

❑ As a Surrounding Influence, grey suggests that everything around you is unclear and confused.

❑ As an Obstacle, grey indicates that until you can think clearly, you mustn't make any decisions.

❑ In the Past position, grey signifies that confusion reigned regarding the matter under question.

❑ In the Present position, the color denotes that confusion over the matter at hand has led to feelings of fear and despondency.

❑ As an Outcome or in a Future position, the indication is that the outlook is not clear and can go in many directions. It is likely to remain clouded until you take the steps needed to clear the air.

MATERIAL

This is not the time for decisions, changes, or any type of action. You would be smart to delay any decisions.

❑ As a Surrounding Influence, grey suggests you're encircled by a heavy cloud cover. Proceed with caution.

❑ As an Obstacle, grey indicates that the confused state of matters is hindering any progress.

❑ In the Past position, the color shows everything was chaotic. However, the confusion and despondency are now in the past.

❑ If grey appears in the Present position, chaos reigns. Matters are so clouded that any action would be foolhardy. Wait until the confusion clears.

❑ As an Outcome or in a Future position, grey means that the matter under consideration will lead to confusion and despondency. Take action to avoid that outcome.

SPIRITUAL

When grey appears in this position it indicates that any pursuit of spiritual matters is surrounded by confusion and misunderstanding. Fear may be a factor here.

❑ As a Surrounding Influence, grey signifies that your search is heavily clouded. Your confusion only leads to misunderstanding. You should consider removing yourself from your situation.

❑ As an Obstacle, grey indicates that your spiritual pursuits are not clear. Confusion and misunderstanding block your progress.

❑ In the Past position, grey shows that your spiritual quest was under a cloud.

❑ In the Present position, you are engulfed in confusion and fear regarding any spiritual matters.

❑ As an Outcome or in a Future position, grey suggests that the path you are following leads to confusion or despondency. You need to reroute your thinking.

★ ★ ★

There is no intensified grey.

WHITE

COLOR KEYS: Insightful awareness. Realization. Protection. Understanding reached through clear and positive thinking.

EMOTIONAL

You've attained an understanding of your emotions. You can approach your feelings in an unemotional way, which allows you to see them clearly. Relationships hold no surprises. What you see is what you get.

❑ If white appears as a Surrounding Influence, the indication is that you already understand the basis of your concern.

❑ If white appears in the Obstacle position, you may be too emotionally detached. Setting yourself apart in order to understand a situation may not be the right approach. Put more feeling into the matter.

❑ In the Past position, white shows that the evidence was there. You might have reached an understanding.

❑ In the Present position, the color signifies that you're on the right track. Matters are clearing.

❑ As an Outcome or in a Future position, white reveals that you'll be surrounded by the white light of understanding and protection. The path is clear; you can reach your goals.

MATERIAL

Things are clearing up around you. You will have to deal with everything out in the open now. This is the only way to achieve success. White generally indicates a positive result regarding finances, careers, or other material matters.

❏ As an Obstacle, white indicates that you may be approaching the matter in a cold, unemotional way. The oracle is reminding you that all that glitters is not gold. Use your intuition.

❏ In the Past position, white signifies that you were seeing matters clearly, and had achieved an understanding.

❏ In the Present position, white indicates that the matter under concern is now out in the open. You're dealing with it. You've made the right decision.

❏ If white appears as an Outcome or in one of the Future positions, it means that the road ahead is clear and positive. You will have the understanding to achieve whatever you want.

SPIRITUAL

The white light of protection surrounds you and your beliefs. Your quest for the truth allows you to penetrate the darkness. You clearly see the undesirable aspects of any philosophy or religion.

❏ As a Surrounding Influence, white suggests that the factors are favorable for you to proceed with any matters of spiritual growth.

❏ As an Obstacle, white indicates that a cold, unemotional approach to any philosophy is wrong. The basis of every religious philosophy is love. The oracle advises you to allow your feelings to flow freely.

❏ In the Past position, white shows that you have reached an understanding of life. The question is: What have you done with it?

❏ In the Present position, white implies that you are being guided in your seeking.

❏ As an Outcome or in a Future position, white signifies that if you keep to your path, you will achieve the understanding you are seeking.

There is no intensified white.

BLACK

COLOR KEYS: Hidden thoughts, feelings, or actions. Something that's not presently being revealed.

EMOTIONAL

There is something hidden. Either you or someone else is hiding his or her feelings. You're not getting the full story. If the question pertains to a relationship, there's something not being said by one of you. The oracle suggests that a heart-to-heart talk is needed.

❑ As a Surrounding Influence, black indicates that hidden thoughts or feelings are affecting the matter in question.

❑ As an Obstacle, the indication is that secret thoughts or feelings are blocking you from resolving your concern.

❑ In the Past position, black shows that emotions were concealed, not allowing you to resolve your situation.

❑ In the Present position, black signifies that right now what you are asking about can't be revealed. The answer is hidden.

❑ If you roll black as an Outcome or in a Future position, it means that the situation will remain unresolved. There is no way at this time to ascertain what the future will hold. For example, a secret romance will remain secret.

MATERIAL

Black indicates something hidden, undetected, or ignored. For example, if you're involved with any kind of contract, you'd be advised to read the small print carefully.

❑ As a Surrounding Influence, black indicates that whatever is being kept from you is playing a role in the matter under question.

❑ As an Obstacle, black indicates that hidden influences are blocking you from achieving your objective.

❑ In the Past position, black signifies that hidden actions have affected the matter in question.

❑ If black appears in the Present position, it means that the matter under question is hidden. Wait awhile. The answer may soon be apparent.

❑ As an Outcome or in a Future position, black implies that a secret or hidden matter will be the result.

SPIRITUAL

Secret matters. Hidden knowledge. The connotation of black is not necessarily negative. However, what is hidden or unknown is often a source of fear, and fear implies negativity.

❑ Black as a Surrounding Influence suggests that hidden matters abound in your search.

❑ As an Obstacle, whatever is hidden is serving to block your path. Try to shed light on whatever it is.

❑ In the Past position, black indicates that something unseen was affecting your spiritual search.

❑ In the Present position, black signifies that a secret matter or something hidden is playing a role in your search. If you are involved with other people in a religious group or cult, find out what is hidden. Don't be manipulated by secret knowledge that is held out like a magic wand. There are other ways of attaining what you seek.

❑ As an Outcome or in a Future position, black indicates the result of your quest is unknown at this time. There is not enough knowledge or understanding to know what the outcome will be.

There is no intensified black.

RAINBOW

COLOR KEYS: Free will. Adaptability. A lucky streak.

EMOTIONAL

You run the gamut from positive to negative and all the different levels in between. The rainbow represents a lucky streak that allows you the adaptability to adjust to any situation in which you find yourself. In a relationship, if you stay flexible, you'll never find yourself bored.

❏ As a Surrounding Influence, the rainbow implies that you have a variety of choices available to you, and it is your job to select one that suits you.

❏ As an Obstacle, the rainbow indicates that your emotional shifts are blocking you from attaining what you want.

❏ In the Past position, the rainbow signifies that you were adaptable and adjusted well to all situations.

❏ In the Present position, the rainbow suggests that your flexibility is allowing you to accomplish what you want.

❏ As an Outcome or in a Future position, the rainbow suggests that the future holds many choices. Use your free will to decide on your course of action.

MATERIAL

At the end of a rainbow, there is always a pot of gold. If you stay flexible and adjust to any situation, you will always be successful.

❏ As a Surrounding Influence, the rainbow indicates that luck is in the air, and it is up to you to act upon it.

❏ As an Obstacle, the rainbow suggests that you have so many choices before you that you're being blocked by your own unwillingness to make a decision.

❏ In the Past position, the rainbow shows that you have had many opportunities open to you.

❏ In the Present, the rainbow signifies that you are ready to make a choice. Whichever you choose, luck is on your side.

❏ As an Outcome or in a Future position, the rainbow means that the future is full of promise. There may be choices to be made, but the options all lead to the pot of gold.

SPIRITUAL

You take a little bit from each philosophy to make it work for you. An open mind is the only approach you can take. Your free will is more important to you than allegiance to any dogma.

❏ As a Surrounding Influence, the rainbow indicates that many paths are shining brightly.

❏ As an Obstacle, the rainbow implies that there are so many options you're having a hard time making a choice. However, until you do, there can be no advancement.

❏ In the Past position, the rainbow shows that you had many choices presented to you in your spiritual quest. Traditional or established ways didn't bind you. You didn't let them.

❏ In the Present position, the rainbow signifies that you are on the path of your own choosing. The spiritual realm, with all its possibilities, is opening to you.

❏ As an Outcome or as a Future position, the rainbow reveals that you will have the free will and opportunity to pursue your own path to higher knowledge.

★ ★ ★

There is no intensified rainbow.

8
COLOR
COMBINATIONS

Y OU'VE PROBABLY HEARD
the old bromide about the importance of first impressions
when you meet someone new. Those first impressions are
based on intuition, and often turn out to be true. Generally
speaking, the same is true when you throw the color cubes.
The first color rolled should be accepted as the answer.

Still, there are exceptions. Certain colors, such as yellow, grey, and white, may require additional clarification
when they appear in a four- or six-color reading. If you are
unclear about the meaning you received and would like more
information, we suggest rolling an additional cube for clarification. Yellow, grey, and white, when rolled in combination
with another color, create a new meaning. For example, you
would read the combination of grey/green as: Confusion is
caused by resisting change. If the same color appears, such as
grey/grey, it denotes that the meaning of the color is intensified. These same color combinations also apply when two
cubes "accidentally" fall out of your hand during a roll. Here
are the interpretations of the combinations for yellow, grey,
and white. The intensified colors are noted by the capital I (I)
designation.

COLOR COMBINATION CHART 1
YELLOW

Combined with:	By using logic, you...
Red	temper highly emotional matters.
Red (I)	deal with extreme stress.
Orange	reach a balance with your emotions.
Orange (I)	deal with the imbalance of your mind and emotions.
Green	change your status. (See separate Yellow/Green combination commentary under "Other Significant Combinations" section, p. 176.)
Green (I)	deal with deceit and envy.
Blue	find the answer within.
Blue (I)	deal with isolation.
Purple	won't repeat mistakes from the past.
Purple (I)	deal with restrictions.
Pink	are taking the romance out of love.
Pink (I)	confront your worries about the lack of love or health problems.

Combined with:	By using logic, you...
Brown	stabilize your thinking.
Brown (I)	deal with your instability.
Peach	gain contentment.
Violet	avoid the spiritual aspects.
Gold	are achieving your goals.
Silver	aren't stretching your mind enough through fantasy and/or imagination.
White	achieve understanding and take action.
Black	look beyond the obvious for hidden meaning.
Rainbow	decide from the choices before you.

COLOR COMBINATION CHART 2
GREY

Combined with:	Confusion is caused by...
Red	the high energy around you.
Red (I)	stress and extreme emotions.
Orange	a concern about balance.
Orange (I)	an imbalance.
Yellow	intellectualizing everything.
Yellow (I)	your illogical thoughts and actions.
Green	all the changes going on.
Green (I)	resisting change.
Blue	too much internalizing of feelings.
Blue (I)	your isolation.
Purple	too much concern about the past.
Purple (I)	all the restrictions around you.
Pink	concerns over love.
Pink (I)	worries about health or the lack of love.

Combined with:	Confusion is caused by...
Brown	the concern about stability.
Brown (I)	instability.
Peach	being too content.
Violet	lack of spiritual feelings.
Gold	problems with your goals.
Silver	not following your intuitive feelings.
White	a lack of understanding.
Black	something that remains hidden.
Rainbow	too many choices.

COLOR COMBINATION CHART 3
WHITE

Combined with:	You need to understand...
Red	your high level of energy.
Red (I)	your emotions as a cause of stress.
Orange	how to balance your mind and emotions.
Orange (I)	a serious imbalance between your emotional and logical sides
Yellow	the nature of your thoughts.
Yellow (I)	the illogical.
Green	how to deal with changes.
Green (I)	how to deal with deceit or envy.
Blue	your inner self.
Blue (I)	your isolation.
Purple	the past.
Purple (I)	the restrictions around you.
Pink	love.
Pink (I)	more about the condition of your health or prospects for love.

Combined with:	You need to understand...
Brown	the material world.
Brown (I)	feelings of instability.
Peach	how to balance logic and love.
Violet	the spiritual side of yourself.
Gold	your goals.
Silver	your intuition.
Grey	the nature of the confusion surrounding you.
Black	that you must make decisions.
Rainbow	your choices.

OTHER SIGNIFICANT COMBINATIONS

There is a particular significance to the following combinations: Yellow/Green, White/Black, or Black/White. Keep an eye out for these combinations not only when a second roll is made for clarification but when they appear together in a four- or six-color layout, or when two cubes fall out of your hand during a roll.

When these pairings appear in adjoining positions, the color combinations apply to the second position. In other words, if yellow and green were the first two colors you rolled, then you would read yellow/green as the Obstacle. In essence, the Surrounding Influence becomes part of the Obstacle. If yellow/green appears in the third and fourth positions, the combination is read in the fourth (Outcome) position in a four-color reading, or the Present in a six-color reading.

The only positions that don't apply to these color combinations are rolls in the second and third positions. When these colors fall in those positions, ignore them as a combination.

Here are the meanings:

YELLOW/GREEN: This combination denotes legal changes. It can portend either a marriage or a divorce, a change of residence, or a change in jobs.

BLACK/WHITE or WHITE/BLACK: You're in a situation where you have to make a choice. Although you may still be undecided, you must make your choice now.

To see how the combinations work, study these examples. You may remember Delores, the bridge player, from the examples for the six-color readings (Chapter 6, p. 84). In the second (Obstacle) position, two colors fell out of her hand: white/orange. White indicated that her obstacle was an inability to come to an understanding of a matter. However, combined with the orange, the reading became more specific. It indicated that her obstacle was understanding that she needed to balance her emotions with logic.

In the example with Renie (Chapter 6, p. 86), she rolled a yellow/green combination in the fifth position (Future—one to three months). Her question was about her career, and the combination was significant. If yellow had been the only color, it would have indicated that a contract or some other legal matter relating to her career was in the offing. However, yellow/green was more specific. It indicated a change involving legal papers. With a question about a career, it could mean a change of jobs or, possibly, of residence.

9
THE COLOR HOROSCOPE
READING

Т HE COLOR HOROSCOPE
Reading offers a general guide of influences for a one-year
period. It's based on the twelve houses of astrology, which are
explained in a diagram on the opposite page. The colors you
roll represent the influences present in the houses.

The value of understanding these influences is that once
you are aware of them, you have the choice of redirecting
them. In other words, the influences seen through the colors
are not immutable. Any obstacles revealed in the Horoscope
Reading can be overcome. You have free will; the course of
your life is up to you.

THE HOUSES

The first six houses of the horoscope concern personal
matters. The First House deals with the self; the Second
House with resources for the self to use; the Third House
with the mind, which controls the use of the resources; the
Fourth House with a base of operations; the Fifth House with
creative self-expression; and the Sixth House with the means
necessary to carry out the creative thought—work and
health. The last six houses of the horoscope are concerned

MEANINGS OF THE TWELVE HOUSES
OF THE HOROSCOPE

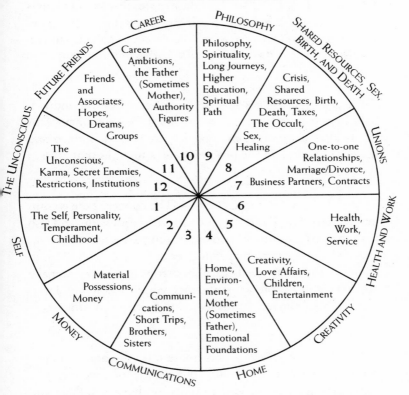

with relationships with other people and with society—how
we react, function, and adapt to the larger world. To help you
to understand the meanings of the twelve houses, we've included a complete description of each one below. For more
details on the houses, we suggest you consult one or more
introductory books on astrology.

FIRST HOUSE: THE SELF—This house represents an individual's basic character. It focuses on self-awareness, how your experiences are assimilated, and how you react to outside stimuli. It also reflects the individual's early environment and conditioning.

SECOND HOUSE: MONEY—The focus here is on the individual's material resources, one's ability to earn money. This house also deals with how you acquire and use money and material goods, and the problems and situations that arise in the process.

THIRD HOUSE: COMMUNICATIONS—The concern here is communication. The Third House deals with expression, and also with the various forms of communicating the written or spoken word: newspapers, magazines, books, radio, television. In addition, this house deals with short trips in which you make contacts with people who influence you or whom you influence. It also concerns brothers and sisters, and other near relatives.

FOURTH HOUSE: HOME—This house rules the home. It concerns our base of operation, our source of security. The Fourth House also deals with one's mother (or father) and one's ability to nurture people emotionally.

FIFTH HOUSE: CREATIVITY—In this house, the focus is creative self-expression, both mental and physical. It deals with the creative arts, especially the performing arts, and also love affairs. In addition, the Fifth House pertains to children, and how you have fun.

SIXTH HOUSE: WORK, HEALTH—This house reveals the individual's attitude about everyday work—the ability to use one's mind in a practical way, and to carry out tasks and responsibilities. One aspect of these responsibilities is the proper care and maintenance of a healthy body.

SEVENTH HOUSE: UNIONS—The focus here is close personal relationships—marriage and partnerships. It also deals with the dissolution of relationships.

EIGHTH HOUSE: SHARED RESOURCES, BIRTH, DEATH, SEX, TAXES, TRANSFORMATION, THE OCCULT—In this house the concern is on jointly held resources. It also deals with death and taxes, wills, the occult, sex, and transformation.

NINTH HOUSE: PHILOSOPHY, HIGHER EDUCATION, SPIRITUALITY—This house concerns philosophy, religion, higher education, and spiritual experiences. It also deals with long journeys, foreign countries, and the law.

TENTH HOUSE: CAREER—The concern here is the individual's base of operation in society—in other words, one's career. The focus is on how ambitious one is, and how the ambitions are carried out. It also concerns the father (or mother).

ELEVENTH HOUSE: FRIENDS—This house deals with group creative expression—the ability to form group associations and to make friends. The focus is on how the individual goes about forming these relationships. This house also deals with hopes and dreams.

TWELFTH HOUSE: THE UNCONSCIOUS, KARMA—This house rules the unconscious mind, memories, and emotional experiences. It can also deal with meditation and mystical inspiration. In addition, it concerns secret enemies, limitations, and societal institutions.

LAYING OUT A COLOR HOROSCOPE READING

Begin by clarifying in your mind the period of time you are inquiring about. No specific question need be asked. Roll the cubes as you would with the other kinds of Rainbow Readings, but now mentally say the name of the house with each roll. For example, your first roll will be The Self; the second roll, Money; the third, Communications.

After each roll, write down the colors according to the number of each house as you roll. When you've completed your rolls and are interpreting the meanings, you may want further information on a color in a particular house. In that case, you can throw another cube for clarification. Jot down the color next to the one you're seeking to clarify.

The interpretations are listed according to color, with the meanings of each of the Twelve Houses presented under each color. The intensified hues are summarized at the end of each section on the individual colors.

While two or more aspects appear in each house, not all of them necessarily apply. For example, if you don't have any brothers or sisters, that section of the Third House won't apply to you. Also, be aware of the subtle differences in the meanings of various aspects. While "work" appears in the Sixth House, "career" is found in the Tenth House. Likewise, while "sex" is discussed in the Eighth House, "love affairs" are the domain of the Fifth House.

COLOR HOROSCOPE INTERPRETATIONS

RED

FIRST HOUSE: THE SELF

You are a high-energy person, and as a result you may find yourself experiencing surges of energy from time to time in the coming months. You must keep moving to stay on top of events. Everything around you may appear to be unfolding at a rapid pace.

SECOND HOUSE: MONEY

There will be lots of activity related to finances—money coming in, money going out. There could be unexpected expenses. Be cautious with investments.

THIRD HOUSE: COMMUNICATIONS, SHORT JOURNEYS, BROTHERS, SISTERS

There will be a tendency to act impulsively in response to what others tell you. Don't overreact.

You'll have opportunities for short journeys on the spur of the moment, but don't count on them to be relaxing.

There are strong emotional interactions with brothers and sisters.

FOURTH HOUSE: HOME, ENVIRONMENT, MOTHER (OR FATHER)

The home will provide a source of your energy, but be aware that there won't be much time to relax.

The mother/father is an intense person with an abundance of energy. The identified parent is highly emotional.

You may be feeling his/her influence in the coming months.

FIFTH HOUSE: CREATIVITY, LOVE AFFAIRS, CHILDREN

Be prepared for high-energy situations in creative endeavors. You may have little time for diversion from your work in the coming months. Be aware that you cannot always force the results you're seeking.

Love affairs will be intense, passionate. However, they may not be long-lived. When the flames die, there's little left.

There may be volatile relationships with a child or children. It's up to you to defuse these situations as they occur. Turn the high energy in positive directions.

SIXTH HOUSE: WORK, HEALTH

Expect circumstances to develop in work situations that require intense concentration. If you're operating at a moderate pace now, you'll be shifting into high gear in the coming months.

In terms of health, you are strong and full of energy. Lots of physical action is foreseen in the coming months. Learn to relax and take things in stride. It'll be the best way to protect yourself.

SEVENTH HOUSE: MARRIAGE, BUSINESS PARTNERSHIPS, CONTRACTS

A marriage in the next twelve months would be intensely emotional and physical. The flames of passion rise.

Any type of partnership or contract formed in the coming months will very likely be forged under highly emotional circumstances.

If divorce is being contemplated during the coming months, expect emotions to run high.

EIGHTH HOUSE: SHARED RESOURCES, BIRTH, DEATH, TAXES, THE OCCULT, SEX

Caution is needed regarding shared money and resources during the coming months. Surging emotions could cause complications.

A birth or death generates high emotions.

Concerning occult interests, high energy puts you in touch with the unconscious mind. Positive thinking will prevent you from being too gullible.

Sexual experiences are intense. There is a preoccupation with sexual matters.

NINTH HOUSE: PHILOSOPHY, SPIRITUALITY, HIGHER EDUCATION, LONG JOURNEYS

As long as you can keep your attention and your energy focused on the search for knowledge, your efforts will yield results.

Your approach to spirituality is highly energetic. Time and patience will bring you what you seek. Don't be too emotional.

Long journeys during this period would not be rewarding. A trip being planned might be unexpectedly canceled.

TENTH HOUSE: CAREER, FATHER (OR MOTHER)

Events affecting your career occur in rapid sequence. Be careful not to overreact to emotionally charged circumstances. Make good use of your high level of energy in the coming months.

Matters related to the father/mother or authority figure could be emotional. There's a need to communicate. If arguments erupt, you need to control yourself.

ELEVENTH HOUSE: FRIENDS, HOPES, DREAMS, GROUPS

During the coming months, your high energy can forge new friendships or group associations that can prove beneficial for all involved.

Surging emotions raise your hopes. But don't take any steps you can't justify logically. Your dreams can be achieved with patience.

TWELFTH HOUSE: THE UNCONSCIOUS, KARMA, SECRET ENEMIES, RESTRICTIONS, INSTITUTIONS

Your unconscious is charged with energy. You can use this energy to draw upon deeper levels of awareness. Learn to discriminate between negative and positive impulses.

Your karmic lessons are extremely emotional.

Be aware that your level of energy and action could cause envy and result in secret enemies.

You react to restrictions emotionally. Don't let your emotions get the better of you. Once you're aware of your limitations, you can overcome them.

There may be emotional encounters in the coming months related to your contact with institutions.

RED (INTENSIFIED)—ALL HOUSES

When the color is intensified, you find yourself becoming too emotionally involved. Stress runs rampant. High levels of energy are expended in anger and hostility. When the warning signal of intensified red appears, it's time to cool down by adding the light of understanding to whatever concerns you.

ORANGE

First House: The Self
You are achieving a healthy balance between your emotions and your mind.

Second House: Money
The financial picture remains balanced or achieves balance in the coming months. There is no reason for alarm.

Third House: Communications, Short Journeys, Brothers, Sisters
The best way to achieve a balance of the emotions and logic is by communicating with those involved. Be aware that cutting off others may place matters out of balance.

Short journeys will provide you with a chance to relax and give you perspective on matters.

Relations are balanced with brothers and sisters.

Fourth House: Home, Environment, Mother (or Father)
At home and elsewhere, everything will seem synchronized.

The mother (or father) is well balanced.

Fifth House: Creativity, Love Affairs, Children
In the coming months you will have the ability to bring all your creative ideas to fruition. Act while the time is ripe.

Regarding love affairs, passion is tempered by logic. As you reach this balance, be aware that some of the spontaneity may be lost. But the spark is still there.

You will gain a balanced perspective concerning the children involved in your life. Have faith in them.

SIXTH HOUSE: WORK, HEALTH

In matters related to your job, things should work out well for you in the coming months. Remember to balance your priorities.

In regard to your health, you're suffused with vitality.

SEVENTH HOUSE: MARRIAGE, BUSINESS PARTNERSHIPS, CONTRACTS

A marriage in the coming months has the potential to provide a well-balanced relationship.

Success in any partnership or contract seems likely. Your abilities are balanced by your partners.

If divorce is being considered, remember that no problem is so great that it can't be overcome by the right approach.

EIGHTH HOUSE: SHARED RESOURCES, BIRTH, DEATH, TAXES, THE OCCULT, SEX

Regarding shared money and resources, you need to keep a balanced perspective in the coming months. Consider the other person's needs as well as your own.

You will most likely take a practical approach to any birth or death affecting you.

In occult matters, you will consider the scientific as well as the metaphysical approach.

Your sexual expression is balanced—a little love, a little romance, a little logic.

NINTH HOUSE: PHILOSOPHY, SPIRITUALITY, HIGHER EDUCATION, LONG JOURNEYS

The pursuit of a basic philosophy of life, and the practical application of it, keep you in good stead and show you your spiritual path.

A long journey could offset the stress you may be feeling at home or on the job.

TENTH HOUSE: CAREER, FATHER (OR MOTHER)

Your career has come together, and you should move ahead now with few barriers.

The father (or mother) is supportive and understanding.

ELEVENTH HOUSE: FRIENDS, HOPES, DREAMS, GROUPS

Close friends and groups help keep you in balance.

You maintain a good balance of fantasy and reality in your hopes and dreams.

TWELFTH HOUSE: THE UNCONSCIOUS, KARMA, SECRET ENEMIES, RESTRICTIONS, INSTITUTIONS

You are balanced at the unconscious level. Reinforce the positive aspects in your life.

Your karmic path is to achieve a balance between the mind and the emotions.

Restrictions don't exist for you if you remain true to your basic feelings and look at them logically.

Seek to settle any conflicts with institutions through the use of logic and intuition.

ORANGE (INTENSIFIED)—ALL HOUSES

You fall off balance, tending to move too deeply into the emotional or the logical side. All your responses are thrown into a state of imbalance.

YELLOW

FIRST HOUSE: THE SELF

Logic and intellect will see you through any rough times in the months ahead. Curb your emotions.

SECOND HOUSE: MONEY

Money-making opportunities may arise through legal documents in the coming months. Use your logic in all transactions.

THIRD HOUSE: COMMUNICATIONS, SHORT JOURNEYS, BROTHERS, SISTERS

Correspondence of some type will lead to a contract or legal document during the coming months.

Short journeys will provide opportunities. Take advantage of them by keeping your eyes open.

You see the bright side of brothers and sisters.

FOURTH HOUSE: HOME, ENVIRONMENT, MOTHER (OR FATHER)

Home is a logical place for you. Your environment is important for clear thinking as long as emotional entanglements don't clutter your thoughts.

The mother (or father) is a bright, clear thinker. The parent weighs carefully all that is said. However, although her or his advice may be sound, it may not always be the best course for you to follow.

FIFTH HOUSE: CREATIVITY, LOVE AFFAIRS, CHILDREN

The coming months will be the time to make all your creative ideas a reality. Put your life in order. Take any necessary legal steps.

In the year ahead, look carefully at all relationships and put more emotion into them. Then you'll be able to see past your logic.

Children are a bright spot. Use your logic in dealing with any minor problems.

SIXTH HOUSE: WORK, HEALTH

In your work, changes for the better are coming to pass. There could be a promotion or a clearing up of a misunderstanding.

Regarding your health for the coming months, you are physically in tune.

SEVENTH HOUSE: MARRIAGE, BUSINESS PARTNERSHIPS, CONTRACTS

If you are single, marriage is a possibility during the coming months.

Regarding partnerships or contracts, the time is right. Yellow is the best color for any matter related to contracts. Partnerships will be orderly and efficient, but they probably won't be very emotional. You and your partner will emphasize logic in the solution to problems.

Any divorce that would occur in the coming months would be a logical matter, devoid of emotion. You sign the papers, everything falls into order. The passion, anguish, and anger are all in the past.

EIGHTH HOUSE: SHARED RESOURCES, BIRTH, DEATH, TAXES, THE OCCULT, SEX

Regarding shared money, use your logic. Everything should be put into a contract. Make sure all parties understand the details.

In matters related to death, legal concerns may arise. Make sure everything is in order to prevent problems later on. You look upon a birth as a bright experience, a ray of hope.

Regarding the occult, you take a scientific approach. You want proof before you commit yourself. It's only logical.

You approach sex more intellectually than emotionally. You are the scientist conducting experiments.

NINTH HOUSE: PHILOSOPHY, SPIRITUALITY, HIGHER EDUCATION, LONG JOURNEYS

Yellow is closely associated with matters of the higher mind and education. There is no limit to what you can achieve. Your approach to spiritual and philosophical matters is strictly logical. It has to make sense.

If long journeys are planned, check carefully for problems with tickets, reservations, or other details. Don't travel without verification of all plans.

TENTH HOUSE: CAREER, FATHER (OR MOTHER)

Regarding your career, education will play a key role. There may also be some form of recognition coming in the months ahead.

The father (or mother) is an excellent resource for a clear, concise opinion that won't be cluttered by emotion.

ELEVENTH HOUSE: FRIENDS, HOPES, DREAMS, GROUPS

You can learn a lot from your friends and group associations. Look toward others for support and guidance.

Education holds the key to your hopes and dreams. The more learned, the more earned.

TWELFTH HOUSE: THE UNCONSCIOUS, KARMA, SECRET ENEMIES, RESTRICTIONS, INSTITUTIONS

You are like a sponge soaking up everything you encounter. Your unconscious mind shines through. Keep your thoughts positive and you'll succeed.

Your karmic path is to put aside your emotions and reach for solutions through logic.

Understanding limitations allows you to overcome them. Secret enemies don't have much impact. You don't allow emotional concerns to take the upper hand.

Matters with institutions should be handled with logic. You may receive a contract or legal document related to an institution. Examine it carefully.

YELLOW (INTENSIFIED)—ALL HOUSES

Logic is taken to an extreme. You may be too rigid and unemotional. Too much order and logic stifle creative thought and actions. Inquiry is displaced by suspicion.

GREEN

FIRST HOUSE: THE SELF

During the coming months you will be like a chameleon, changing colors to fit your environment.

SECOND HOUSE: MONEY

Changes in your financial status are likely in the coming months. Expect small gains, usually related to fresh starts.

THIRD HOUSE: COMMUNICATIONS, SHORT JOURNEYS, BROTHERS, SISTERS

You can change things in the coming months by clearly communicating what you want. It could involve making a request in writing, or some other form of communication.

Short journeys promote growth. A change in attitude brought on by a trip may help you see things more clearly. Also, you might make new friends or allies who will aid you in your endeavors.

Brothers and sisters are changing, growing. Your attitudes about them may be shifting.

FOURTH HOUSE: HOME, ENVIRONMENT, MOTHER (OR FATHER)

The home will be a place of change, growth, and renewal in the next twelve months.

The mother or father is a nurturer. The parent's influence can promote growth.

FIFTH HOUSE: CREATIVITY, LOVE AFFAIRS, CHILDREN

Fresh, innovative ideas during the coming months can work favorably for you.

If you're involved in a love affair, there will be an opportunity for a more positive relationship. If you're not presently involved in a relationship, a new one is due in the near future.

Growth will be the key word in your relationship with children. Small changes are due. Be firm, but don't stifle.

SIXTH HOUSE: WORK, HEALTH

The coming months should bring small changes related to your work. There may be more money, a promotion, or a new start of some kind.

You will undergo a healing of sorts during the coming months. It may give you a new lease on life.

SEVENTH HOUSE: MARRIAGE, BUSINESS PARTNERSHIPS, CONTRACTS

Your marriage will be a place of growth and healing during the coming months. If you're considering a divorce, try making a fresh start with your spouse. Learn from your past mistakes.

New ideas emerge from a partnership or contract during the coming months.

EIGHTH HOUSE: SHARED RESOURCES, BIRTH, DEATH, TAXES, THE OCCULT, SEX

Small improvements in shared finances are in store. The

coming months will be a fruitful time for entering a joint venture.

Death marks the end of the old and the beginning of the new. The phoenix rising from the ashes is an apt symbol—a new birth.

A growth of interest or a change in attitude regarding the occult is at hand in the coming months. A positive perspective will reap positive results.

Your attitudes toward sex are flexible and may change. Anything new and appealing can change your thinking.

NINTH HOUSE: PHILOSOPHY, SPIRITUALITY, HIGHER EDUCATION, LONG JOURNEYS

Educational endeavors will generate the flow of new ideas. Remain flexible to allow for growth.

You are on the path to philosophical and spiritual growth.

Regarding plans for long journeys, a fresh start may be in store. Scout around for new possibilities.

TENTH HOUSE: CAREER, FATHER (OR MOTHER)

Changes may be in store for you regarding your career. Clear away the cobwebs and watch for fresh ideas. They may generate new possibilities. A new approach to a matter of importance may well gain widespread acceptance.

The father (or mother) may be deeply involved with changes in your life.

ELEVENTH HOUSE: FRIENDS, HOPES, DREAMS, GROUPS

Expect new friends to enter your life in the coming

months. Now is the time to evaluate your life and plant seeds for the future. Involvement with groups may prove to be fertile ground.

Hopes or dreams, which seem like a diversion, will blossom into something more. Watch it grow.

TWELFTH HOUSE: THE UNCONSCIOUS, KARMA, SECRET ENEMIES, RESTRICTIONS, INSTITUTIONS

Your unconscious is a source of growth and inspiration. You're always looking for a new start.

Your karmic lesson is to overcome any fear of change.

Secret enemies may envy your resourcefulness.

Regarding restrictions, you have a tendency to become bored with repetitive actions.

Dealings with institutions will generate money for you.

GREEN (INTENSIFIED)—ALL HOUSES

Change may not be a good idea in the coming months. Be careful of ideas you plant in your mind. You may be on the wrong track. Too many changes result in chaos.

BLUE

FIRST HOUSE: THE SELF

You're a private person, a loner. You hold things back and keep inner turmoil to yourself. On the surface, you radiate peace, keeping the turmoil within.

SECOND HOUSE: MONEY

You may face a financial lull in the coming months. Use the time wisely. Plan ahead and follow your inner feelings.

THIRD HOUSE: COMMUNICATIONS, SHORT JOURNEYS, BROTHERS, SISTERS

Too much communicating wears you out. Stay private as much as possible in the coming months. Let your thoughts be your own. Quiet weekends will benefit you. Plan ahead.

Brothers and sisters are a source of inner peace.

FOURTH HOUSE: HOME, ENVIRONMENT, MOTHER (OR FATHER)

Stay close to home as much as possible during the coming months. You will gain strength from your surroundings and loved ones.

The mother (or father) radiates a deep love. Nevertheless, the parent is very private. Don't crowd her (or him).

FIFTH HOUSE: CREATIVITY, LOVE AFFAIRS, CHILDREN

You have a hard time expressing yourself. Your ideas are worthwhile, but you feel insecure when explaining them.

You keep your feelings about the one you love locked up. You must learn to express all that you feel. Your fantasies may be more exciting than your actual sex life.

Children will be a source of inner satisfaction in the coming months.

SIXTH HOUSE: WORK, HEALTH

Regarding your work, things are at an even keel and will remain that way. Expect no highs or lows in the coming months. However, if you want things to change—speak up!

.Any ailments you contract during the coming months may well be psychosomatic. They develop from conflicts within you. That, however, doesn't mean they are any less real. Try not to create such problems for yourself.

SEVENTH HOUSE: MARRIAGE, BUSINESS PARTNERSHIPS, CONTRACTS

If you are married or contemplating marriage, you should open up more and share your feelings. It will bolster the relationship. The only danger with your relationship in the coming months is your own self-centered thinking. Take a look around you and count your blessings.

Regarding partnerships, someone who is different from you will stimulate the partnership and motivate you. Before signing a contract, carefully contemplate your options. A contract can bring peace of mind.

A divorce in the coming months may result in peace of mind. You might be somewhat isolated by it.

EIGHTH HOUSE: SHARED RESOURCES, BIRTH, DEATH, TAXES, THE OCCULT, SEX

In matters of shared resources, you may see a quiet period in the coming months. Make sure you clearly communicate your thoughts and feelings. It will ease the strain.

You feel a sense of peace and tranquility regarding a birth or death.

Follow your feelings regarding occult matters. Peace comes from within.

Your sex life is a bit inhibited but intense. You are very private about sexual matters.

NINTH HOUSE: PHILOSOPHY, SPIRITUALITY, HIGHER EDUCATION, LONG JOURNEYS

Seek answers from within. Your inner self guides you in spiritual or philosophical matters. However, don't be surprised if you find yourself asking advice from someone whose judgment you trust.

Plan carefully for long journeys.

TENTH HOUSE: CAREER, FATHER (OR MOTHER)

The coming months will be the right time to act on your secret goals. Since you are such a private person, you don't care for the fanfare that comes with success in your career. You subconsciously avoid the recognition that others actively seek.

The father (or mother) is a quiet, private person, not one to express his/her feelings. But don't sell him/her short, his/her feelings are intense.

ELEVENTH HOUSE: FRIENDS, HOPES, DREAMS, GROUPS

In order to make friendships, you must go out of your way and force yourself to be more expressive. Even loners need friends. Group associations will help achieve this goal.

You're a dreamer, and you procrastinate about turning your hopes into reality. You need to be more aggressive.

TWELFTH HOUSE: THE UNCONSCIOUS, KARMA, SECRET ENEMIES, RESTRICTIONS, INSTITUTIONS

You draw a sense of tranquility and peace from your unconscious well of knowledge.

Your karmic lesson is to achieve peace of mind.

You can be your own worst "secret enemy." You erect barriers you find hard to leap over.

In the coming months, there will be some sort of gain for you related to an institution, such as a hospital.

BLUE (INTENSIFIED)—ALL HOUSES

Your feelings are trapped inside, causing loneliness, depression, and isolation. You're not able to express yourself.

PURPLE

FIRST HOUSE: THE SELF

You are a romantic person tied to the past. You tend to set limits on yourself and find it hard to accept the new.

SECOND HOUSE: MONEY

In money matters, stick to what you know. There are rules and regulations around you that will be present for another three months.

THIRD HOUSE: COMMUNICATIONS, SHORT JOURNEYS, BROTHERS, SISTERS

Don't expect everything to be revealed through a letter or any other means of communication. You will receive only a limited version of what is.

Regarding short journeys, traveling should be restricted to places that you know.

Brothers and sisters are reminders of the past. You act accordingly.

FOURTH HOUSE: HOME, ENVIRONMENT, MOTHER (OR FATHER)

You surround yourself with what is familiar and comfortable. Your home is a cocoon of the past, and reinforces the limitations you place upon yourself.

The mother (or father) will always see you as a child and therefore may restrict your growth in some ways.

FIFTH HOUSE: CREATIVITY, LOVE AFFAIRS, CHILDREN

You need to emerge from the past and combine what you know with more immediate or futuristic ideas. The combination will amaze you.

Regarding love affairs, you tend to be a romantic. However, you have a tendency to repeat mistakes you've made in the past. Make sure you look back and compare your past actions with your present ones. Don't get hung up on restrictions.

Don't place too many rules and regulations around the children in your life. Allow them room to grow.

SIXTH HOUSE: WORK, HEALTH

Regarding your work, be careful not to fall into the same traps that spelled trouble for you in the past. Be more flexible and open to the suggestions of others.

If you've been healthy, you will remain so. If certain ailments seem chronic, a more positive attitude would help a great deal.

SEVENTH HOUSE: MARRIAGE, BUSINESS PARTNERSHIPS, CONTRACTS

You approach marriage as a set routine to be followed. Be aware that your marriage can be either romantic or restrictive. It's up to you. Be guided by the lessons you've learned in the past. A divorce in the coming months might be a repeat of the past. Consider it carefully.

You see any partnership or contract as harboring restrictions. You place it in a certain perspective and religiously follow a set pattern.

EIGHTH HOUSE: SHARED RESOURCES, BIRTH, DEATH, TAXES, THE OCCULT, SEX

In matters of shared money or resources, you tend to place limits on what can be gained by such relationships. Examine these thoughts carefully. You can overcome all self-imposed limitations.

Regarding death, release the fear of it and you will have no problems. Births are reminders of the past.

Concerning the occult, don't accept any restrictions or limitations imposed by others. Remember, you are the only true guru in your life.

Your attitude about sex is very traditional. You are set in your ways. You create your own limitations.

NINTH HOUSE: PHILOSOPHY, SPIRITUALITY, HIGHER EDUCATION, LONG JOURNEYS

Your concepts of philosophy and spirituality are cluttered with rigid ideas. The confines of your religious upbringing may have created restrictions in your thoughts. Relying too heavily on the past could make the difference between continued restrictions and a new sense of freedom. Keep in mind the lessons from earlier years, but don't cling to the past.

You will find a long journey more rewarding if it is within familiar territory.

TENTH HOUSE: CAREER, FATHER (OR MOTHER)

Professionally, you function within a tight, inflexible circle, which prevents others from recognizing your accomplishments. Loosen up. Set new goals. Reach for more in your career.

The father (or mother) is ruled by the past. The parent may be unyielding at times.

ELEVENTH HOUSE: FRIENDS, HOPES, DREAMS, GROUPS

Old friends are steadfast. You repeat past patterns in your relationships with groups.

Your hopes and dreams are outdated. They need revision.

TWELFTH HOUSE: THE UNCONSCIOUS, KARMA, SECRET ENEMIES, RESTRICTIONS, INSTITUTIONS

The unconscious mind holds knowledge from the past. When you learn to draw the unconscious into your everyday awareness, it will provide inspiration. But you must separate the restrictive from the constructive.

Your karmic lesson is to put aside restrictions from the past and start anew.

This is the color of self-imposed restrictions. Awareness of that fact will allow you to step beyond rules and regulations that are too confining. In the coming months you are offered the opportunity to act as a free thinker.

Past ties with institutions could serve you well. Positive thinking should be emphasized. Don't overindulge in past associations.

PURPLE (INTENSIFIED)—ALL HOUSES

The characteristics associated with each house are carried to an extreme. Past actions hinder your growth. Restrictions and limitations surround you. It's emphatically important for you to break the chains that bind you to the past.

PINK

FIRST HOUSE: THE SELF

You are a dedicated romantic. You literally glow with a sense of health and vitality.

SECOND HOUSE: MONEY

Any financial problems will be cleared up in the coming months, especially if you maintain a positive outlook.

THIRD HOUSE: COMMUNICATIONS, SHORT JOURNEYS, BROTHERS, SISTERS

You may receive letters or other forms of communication containing a romantic twist.

Short journeys may offer romantic interludes in the coming months.

Brothers and sisters are a healthy influence on you.

FOURTH HOUSE: HOME, ENVIRONMENT, MOTHER (OR FATHER)

Concentrate on healthy activities in the home. Exercise and a proper diet during the next months will benefit you.

The mother (or father) is a loving parent who can be extremely helpful.

FIFTH HOUSE: CREATIVITY, LOVE AFFAIRS, CHILDREN

Ideas will come to you quickly and easily in the next few months. You can make use of many of them.

Romance will be uppermost in your mind. The love that you give is returned tenfold.

Regarding children, their good upbringing shows. They are vital and healthy.

SIXTH HOUSE: WORK, HEALTH

By staying vital and in tune with what is happening around you at work, you are rewarded.

A clean bill of health is in store for you, especially if you exercise regularly and maintain a good diet.

SEVENTH HOUSE: MARRIAGE, BUSINESS PARTNERSHIPS, CONTRACTS

Keeping romance alive makes for a healthy marriage in the next months. If you are single, marriage or a vital relationship may soon be in your future. If you are considering a divorce, keep in mind that a new love may be the same as the old one.

A partnership or contract may work well for you in the coming months, especially if you share responsibilities fairly.

EIGHTH HOUSE: SHARED RESOURCES, BIRTH, DEATH, TAXES, THE OCCULT, SEX

Matters of shared resources will work out well for you in the next months, providing the relationship between the partners remains an amicable one.

A more positive attitude about a birth or death will clear up any stress you feel.

Keep an open mind and a healthy outlook regarding any experiences you may have related to occult matters.

Your sexual nature is one that thrives on a loving relationship, not one that is purely sexual.

NINTH HOUSE: PHILOSOPHY, SPIRITUALITY, HIGHER EDUCATION, LONG JOURNEYS

You harbor a love of learning that balances your physical endeavors. You possess the ability to become aware of love in its highest form.

Your spiritual and philosophical outlook are based on love.

Regarding long journeys, a romantic cruise or a trip with a romantic setting would have favorable results.

TENTH HOUSE: CAREER, FATHER (OR MOTHER)

Regarding your career, a healthy mind and body is key to your success.

The father (or mother) is a loving parent who looks at things through rose-colored glasses.

ELEVENTH HOUSE: FRIENDS, HOPES, DREAMS, GROUPS

The friendships you make in coming months will be close ones, and realized through group associations.

Any hopes of a romantic nature for an old friendship are likely to be fulfilled.

TWELFTH HOUSE: THE UNCONSCIOUS, KARMA, SECRET ENEMIES, RESTRICTIONS, INSTITUTIONS

The unconscious is a source of creative energy. A positive outlook will help you achieve all that you desire.

Your karmic lesson is to maintain a healthy attitude and to learn to love yourself as well as others.

A secret enemy might be one whom you once loved.

Settling on one person may seem limiting, but the right person will fulfill your needs.

Institutions dealing with health care or physical fitness may provide you with the opportunities you are seeking.

PINK (INTENSIFIED)—ALL HOUSES

Intensified pink leads to an obsession with health and love. In romance, you may be more in love with love than with any one person, or there may be a lack of love in your life. Others may find you self-centered.

BROWN

FIRST HOUSE: THE SELF

Security is your main goal. You are stable and tend to be steadfast in your decision-making.

SECOND HOUSE: MONEY

The influences around you are geared toward making money. Plant your financial seeds now for material gain.

THIRD HOUSE: COMMUNICATIONS, SHORT JOURNEYS, BROTHERS, SISTERS

When communicating your wishes in the coming months, remain down to Earth. Avoid pretensions.

Travel for financial gain will be favorable during the next months. Look for discounted trips or special fares.

Brothers and sisters represent a sense of stability and security.

FOURTH HOUSE: HOME, ENVIRONMENT, MOTHER (OR FATHER)

Your home is a base of security and stability. You are nurtured in such an environment.

The mother (or father) is down to Earth. The parent described is very security conscious.

FIFTH HOUSE: CREATIVITY, LOVE AFFAIRS, CHILDREN

The practical side of you should be full of activity during the coming months as you put your ideas to work.

A love affair may provide the emotional security you are seeking.

Make sure the children in your life are secure and stable. They tend to be quite materialistic.

SIXTH HOUSE: WORK, HEALTH

A promotion and more money are in store. If you are starting a new business, the prospect is for a stable and secure enterprise.

Your health is stable.

SEVENTH HOUSE: MARRIAGE, BUSINESS PARTNERSHIPS, CONTRACTS

Your marriage is secure, and the outlook is for it to remain that way. Any matters dealing with a divorce are based on materialistic concerns rather than emotions.

Any partnership or contract formed in the next months will work favorably for you.

EIGHTH HOUSE: SHARED RESOURCES, BIRTH, DEATH, TAXES, THE OCCULT, SEX

Shared finances will bring you stability and security during the coming months. Any legal matters will result in stability. There is a possibility of an inheritance through a death during the next months.

You accept a birth or a death as a natural experience— parts of the cycle of life.

You may become aware of a chance to use the occult to assist you in your daily life. By becoming familiar with your inner consciousness, you can develop your intuitive side to your advantage.

Your sexual expression is very earthy.

NINTH HOUSE: PHILOSOPHY, SPIRITUALITY, HIGHER EDUCATION, LONG JOURNEYS

As an Earth-based person, you have the ability to get to the root of things. By studying a matter thoroughly, you gain a solid foundation for material security.

Your approach to philosophical and spiritual matters has a firm foundation.

Any trip that involves you with the outdoors and nature will be revitalizing and worthwhile.

TENTH HOUSE: CAREER, FATHER (OR MOTHER)

You are in an extremely stable period of your career. More money will be generated during the coming months.

The father (or mother) is well grounded and materially oriented. Take the described parent's advice on financial matters.

ELEVENTH HOUSE: FRIENDS, HOPES, DREAMS, GROUPS

Relationships with friends and groups have solid foundations. Some of your friends tend to be materialistic.

Your hopes and dreams are based on financial and emotional security.

TWELFTH HOUSE: THE UNCONSCIOUS, KARMA, SECRET ENEMIES, RESTRICTIONS, INSTITUTIONS

Your unconscious is like the roots of a massive tree. It's

out of view, yet it serves as a foundation and a source of sustenance.

Your karmic lesson is related to dealing with material or emotional security.

Secret enemies might attempt to uproot your stability. As long as you're aware of the possibility, you can deal with it. Restrictions are related to your need for security. You'll do a lot for it, even sacrifice good times.

Any dealings with institutions in the coming months will provide a firm base for you.

BROWN (INTENSIFIED)—ALL HOUSES

All of the qualities above are carried to an extreme. There is too much attention to financial concerns or other material matters. Your overall need for security can hinder you.

PEACH

FIRST HOUSE: THE SELF

You're achieving an inner balance. In the coming months, you may feel mellow and pleasantly relaxed with yourself.

SECOND HOUSE: MONEY

Take advantage of the next twelve months by setting aside some of the extra money you earn. Everything is on the upswing.

THIRD HOUSE: COMMUNICATIONS, SHORT JOURNEYS, BROTHERS, SISTERS

Make it a priority to send out notes or letters or to make calls that express congratulations, thanks, compliments, or whatever is in order. The effort will be appreciated and will be worth your while.

Look for romance during weekend trips.

There's an amiable relationship with brothers and sisters.

FOURTH HOUSE: HOME, ENVIRONMENT, MOTHER (OR FATHER)

You surround yourself with creature comforts as best you can. You seem to thrive amid luxury. The old adage, home is where the heart is, applies to you.

The mother (or father) is a balanced and loving parent. Everything is peachy with the indicated parent.

FIFTH HOUSE: CREATIVITY, LOVE AFFAIRS, CHILDREN

You generate good ideas. Now you need to work on making them practical.

Regarding a love affair, romance is somewhat tempered but still thrives. Your sexual nature calls for love and attention. Without it, life would be empty.

The children in your life are well balanced and warm hearted. Have faith in them.

SIXTH HOUSE: WORK, HEALTH

You have a tendency to be naive regarding your work. Look around you and take stock. Close scrutiny may reveal a few things you've been avoiding.

Proper diet and exercise are called for in order to stay fit and healthy.

SEVENTH HOUSE: MARRIAGE, BUSINESS PARTNERSHIPS, CONTRACTS

Warmth and emotional balance keep your marriage sound. A positive outlook helps. Don't even consider divorce. Any problems can be easily worked out.

Regarding a partnership or contract, the outlook is positive. A balance is achieved.

EIGHTH HOUSE: SHARED RESOURCES, BIRTH, DEATH, TAXES, THE OCCULT, SEX

Energy put forth in the area of shared money and/or resources can multiply rewards.

A realistic view of life could make a big difference regarding any concerns about a birth or death.

In matters of the occult, you can maintain a healthy mind through meditation and positive thinking.

Your attitude toward sex is mellow. Sex is cuddly and warm.

NINTH HOUSE: PHILOSOPHY, SPIRITUALITY, HIGHER EDUCATION, LONG JOURNEYS

A positive and spiritual look at things can make your life happier. Your love of learning is an asset. Use it.

A prolonged rest that combines exercise and play would be ideal.

TENTH HOUSE: CAREER, FATHER (OR MOTHER)

The joy you feel about your career will propel you forward. But don't overlook any details. A happy-go-lucky attitude has pluses and minuses.

The energy of the father (or mother) is never-ending. At times the parent is so busy he/she doesn't take time to look around.

ELEVENTH HOUSE: FRIENDS, HOPES, DREAMS, GROUPS

Your natural love of life will attract the friends you seek. There will be a balance of personalities in any group association.

You are full of hopes and dreams, even though some may be well out of your present grasp.

TWELFTH HOUSE: THE UNCONSCIOUS, KARMA, SECRET ENEMIES, RESTRICTIONS, INSTITUTIONS

Your unconscious mind has reached a state of balance.

At present, you have reached a karmic balance.

Secret enemies may try to catch you off guard. Keep your balance.

Restrictions can be overcome by balancing your logic and emotions.

Your sunny, positive disposition should keep you in good stead. Keep a positive outlook and you will find happiness, even in your dealings with rigidly regulated institutions.

There is no intensified peach.

VIOLET

FIRST HOUSE: THE SELF

You are a spiritual, new era thinker. You are able to rise above the petty aspects of the material world and see a higher order of things.

SECOND HOUSE: MONEY

In the coming months, the need for money will not be an overriding concern. Higher thoughts bring financial success.

THIRD HOUSE: COMMUNICATIONS, SHORT JOURNEYS, BROTHERS, SISTERS

Communication of a higher order is what's in store for you. Staying positively attuned will facilitate such communication.

Weekends of meditation or higher learning will prove successful.

You hold your brothers and sisters in the highest regard.

FOURTH HOUSE: HOME, ENVIRONMENT, MOTHER (OR FATHER)

The home is a sacred province, a sanctuary, a place where you are at peace. The environment is uplifting.

The mother (or father) is a sage or philosopher. Listen well.

FIFTH HOUSE: CREATIVITY, LOVE AFFAIRS, CHILDREN

Your thoughts are of the highest order. A truly aware

person, you have an opportunity to serve mankind.

Love affairs are of a spiritual nature. The deep feelings connecting the two of you create a bond, an awareness that is larger than the sum of the parts.

The children around you are becoming aware of a wider world. Guide them.

SIXTH HOUSE: WORK, HEALTH

In the coming months, it's important that you take your spiritual thoughts and insights and put them to work for you in the everyday world. It will be beneficial for you and others.

A healthy mind and a positive outlook should keep you on an even keel.

SEVENTH HOUSE: MARRIAGE, BUSINESS PARTNERSHIPS, CONTRACTS

You seek higher goals in a marriage than the daily humdrum. If divorce is contemplated in the coming months, the indication is that you are moving on because of concerns of a higher order.

In all partnerships, you should seek a person who is as inclined toward higher deeds as you are. The link will be a strong one. Regarding contracts, maintain a high standard.

EIGHTH HOUSE: SHARED RESOURCES, BIRTH, DEATH, TAXES, THE OCCULT, SEX

In matters of shared resources, you tend to overlook self gain for the larger goals you and your partner have in mind. However, make sure in the months ahead that you protect yourself financially.

Death, like birth, is simply a spiritual renewal, a natural progression.

Regarding the occult, an overall positive view could speed you ahead in your search.

Sex is like a spiritual encounter or psychic experience. You and your partner share other-dimensional adventures through sex.

NINTH HOUSE: PHILOSOPHY, SPIRITUALITY, HIGHER EDUCATION, LONG JOURNEYS

You are striving for a high plateau of spiritual or philosophical awareness. Love and fellowship should come easily for you in the months ahead. Set aside your books, and meditate. Higher knowledge is accessible.

Your life quest is within reach. You'll find the camaraderie you seek in your journey.

TENTH HOUSE: CAREER, FATHER (OR MOTHER)

Regarding your career, the coming months should provide opportunities to help others. You have capabilities of spiritual leadership. Use them wisely. The reward is found within.

The father (or mother) is a wise, spiritual person. Listen carefully to all he or she has to say.

ELEVENTH HOUSE: FRIENDS, HOPES, DREAMS, GROUPS

Friendships will be forged with the higher order of things in mind. Groups you associate with should have universal goals.

Your hopes and dreams in the coming months will increasingly be directed toward gaining a higher awareness.

TWELFTH HOUSE: THE UNCONSCIOUS, KARMA, SECRET ENEMIES, RESTRICTIONS, INSTITUTIONS

Higher understanding is within you. Follow your inner thoughts.

Your karmic lesson is to strive for greater spiritual understanding.

Secret enemies have no impact. You are way beyond them.

Your only course is to help others. Don't consider it a restriction, and it won't be.

You could become involved with alternative types of institutions and organizations that recognize and utilize higher planes of knowledge. They could involve meditative retreats.

There is no intensified violet.

GOLD

FIRST HOUSE: THE SELF

You are goal oriented, an achiever. You are driven, ambitious. A success seeker. You will leave an imprint, make a difference.

SECOND HOUSE: MONEY

You have the Midas touch. Money is not an obstacle.

THIRD HOUSE: COMMUNICATIONS, SHORT JOURNEYS, BROTHERS, SISTERS

In matters of communication, you are a great salesperson. You excel at one-on-one or with mass communications. You will find success in the media—anything related to the written or spoken word.

Brothers and sisters are influential, successful in their own right.

FOURTH HOUSE: HOME, ENVIRONMENT, MOTHER (OR FATHER)

Your home is your castle. You put money into it. It shows who you are, what you are. You set up a glittering facade against which you live your life.

You treasure your mother (or father).

FIFTH HOUSE: CREATIVITY, LOVE AFFAIRS, CHILDREN

You are always looking for innovative ways to capitalize on creativity—yours or others.

You gain financially through love affairs. They are a means to an end and enhance your life.

Children are prompted to achieve. You set high goals for them.

SIXTH HOUSE: WORK, HEALTH

You stay in tip-top shape. Your body is your means of achieving. Your appearance is very important. You put a high value on health and physical fitness. It's all part of the big picture.

Work must always elevate you. It's a stepping-stone. You won't accept a job that doesn't lead to something else.

SEVENTH HOUSE: MARRIAGE, BUSINESS PARTNERSHIPS, CONTRACTS

Gold indicates marriage or a contract is a means of achievement for you. Partnerships must enhance your life or show that you are successful.

If your high ideals are not reached, you could divorce easily. You'd come out smelling like a rose.

You look for perfection in all partnerships. This is an ideal time for signing a contract.

EIGHTH HOUSE: SHARED RESOURCES, BIRTH, DEATH, TAXES, THE OCCULT, SEX

Gain is the key word. There will be profit from shared money.

You will gain from death, such as through an inheritance. A birth is a great success, a time to celebrate.

An interest or involvement in the occult will result in personal gain.

Your sexual expression is goal oriented. Each encounter is viewed as a goal you must achieve.

NINTH HOUSE: PHILOSOPHY, SPIRITUALITY, HIGHER EDUCATION, LONG JOURNEYS

Your philosophical ideas and spiritual approach are geared for positive achievement. You become the ultrapositive thinker. You're oriented to succeed in school. You make education look easy. You're at the top. You're a seeker of perfection.

You gain from long journeys.

TENTH HOUSE: CAREER, FATHER (OR MOTHER)

You are geared to reach the top in your career—if not this month then within a reasonable time. You're ambitious and success oriented. You know no other way.

The father (or mother) has or has had a hand in creating your success, helping to mold your personality.

ELEVENTH HOUSE: FRIENDS, HOPES, DREAMS, GROUPS

Friendships are usually made for personal gain. While this may seem simply expedient to others, it's natural to you.

In any group, you should adopt a leadership role.

You don't just hope. It's not enough. You achieve your dreams.

TWELFTH HOUSE: THE UNCONSCIOUS, KARMA, SECRET ENEMIES, RESTRICTIONS, INSTITUTIONS

Your unconscious is geared to succeed.

Your karmic lesson is to handle success.

Secret enemies would be envious people. You probably wouldn't consider them worthy of your attention.

You don't worry about restrictions. You ignore them.

Your involvement with institutions will lead to successful experiences.

There is no intensified gold.

SILVER

FIRST HOUSE: THE SELF

You are intuitive, extremely sensitive, something of a dreamer.

SECOND HOUSE: MONEY

You are a dreamer. You see how good everything could be, but you're not realistic. Money that comes in quickly during the coming months goes out just as quickly.

THIRD HOUSE: COMMUNICATIONS, SHORT JOURNEYS, BROTHERS, SISTERS

You communicate on a different wavelength during the coming months. It could be spiritual communication.

You're always making short trips, many of which are mental journeys.

You'll be psychically in tune with brothers and sisters.

FOURTH HOUSE: HOME, ENVIRONMENT, MOTHER (OR FATHER)

Your home is an extension of the self, a reflection of your personality or latest philosophies. You have a deep mental link with the mother (or father), a close relationship.

FIFTH HOUSE: CREATIVITY, LOVE AFFAIRS, CHILDREN

You have all the talents to succeed in the creative arts. A lot depends on your initiative.

A love affair in the coming months would be more intense in fantasy than in reality.

There will be good rapport with children, because you are like one yourself.

SIXTH HOUSE: WORK, HEALTH

You might take on a job that appeals to your fantasy life. It would be representative of what you are, who you are.

You maintain a holistic attitude. You believe in a healthy mind in a healthy body.

SEVENTH HOUSE: MARRIAGE, BUSINESS PARTNERSHIPS, CONTRACTS

If you are in search of a lover, the one you seek is someone with depth, usually a person who isn't bogged down by tradition—your soulmate. You need a strong mate to keep you earthbound.

The partnerships or contracts you enter into in the coming months will result from intuitive rather than logical choices. An ideal business partner would be someone who could ground you.

EIGHTH HOUSE: SHARED RESOURCES, BIRTH, DEATH, TAXES, THE OCCULT, SEX

Any shared resources should be entered into with someone who is stable and grounded, who will keep you down to Earth.

A birth is a spiritual experience with karmic implications.

Your approach to death and the occult is metaphysical. There is no fear associated with either. However, you may become preoccupied with the occult. Don't get lost in the clouds.

Sex is your way of forming an emotional link. You tune in on the sexual prowess of others. Your mental trips are sometimes more exciting than the reality.

NINTH HOUSE: PHILOSOPHY, SPIRITUALITY, HIGHER EDUCATION, LONG JOURNEYS

You seek a philosophical and spiritual understanding in your search for the paranormal. You love to travel, and your journeys are adventures in which you might collect legends and lore. You travel to gain knowledge.

TENTH HOUSE: CAREER, FATHER (OR MOTHER)

You may advance in your career in the coming months in unusual ways. You create illusions, like an actor or a writer. You're not everything you seem. Realistically, your ambitions may exceed what you actually accomplish in the coming months.

The relationship with the father (or mother) is nebulous, undefined. The parent is someone who is just there.

ELEVENTH HOUSE: FRIENDS, HOPES, DREAMS, GROUPS

You may make many acquaintances in the coming months, but only a few close friends. You should associate with groups that reflect your goals.

Your hopes exceed all reality. You are a dreamer.

TWELFTH HOUSE: THE UNCONSCIOUS, KARMA, SECRET ENEMIES, RESTRICTIONS, INSTITUTIONS

You have a quick, intuitive mind that draws from your unconscious knowledge.

Your karmic lesson is to understand the intuitive mind and deal with it in a spiritual manner.

Because of your unorthodox ways, you could make secret enemies in the next months.

A major restriction is your tendency to procrastinate.

You might spend some time dealing with an institution. It'll be a temporary arrangement. You won't let it be a lasting one.

There is no intensified silver.

GREY

FIRST HOUSE: THE SELF

There is a sense of confusion within, creating emotional and mental barriers. Don't be too quick to judge yourself. All matters clear in time.

SECOND HOUSE: MONEY

Finances will be a jumble for a short period. Roll again for the outcome.

THIRD HOUSE: COMMUNICATIONS, SHORT JOURNEYS, BROTHERS, SISTERS

Be careful what you say. Your thinking is confused and you could present yourself inaccurately.

Short trips would only be an escape from reality. Stay and face your problems.

You have confused feelings about brothers and sisters.

FOURTH HOUSE: HOME, ENVIRONMENT, MOTHER (OR FATHER)

You need to put your home life in order. There is confusion and disarray around you.

You have mixed feelings about your mother (or father). To work things out, pinpoint the grey areas.

FIFTH HOUSE: CREATIVITY, LOVE AFFAIRS, CHILDREN

You are emotionally and mentally scattered. Your creativity takes many paths. You need to discipline yourself and follow one.

Take each day as it comes, and remember that love conquers all.

Children are a source of confusion.

SIXTH HOUSE: WORK, HEALTH

Your work needs more clarification. Get rid of the confusion.

Too much confusion makes one forget that a healthy mind creates a healthy body.

SEVENTH HOUSE: MARRIAGE, BUSINESS PARTNERSHIPS, CONTRACTS

A union could be made happier if you make up your mind about what you want from a spouse or a partner.

To think of divorce or detachment only adds confusion.

Be wary of any proposal or contracts. It is not advisable to sign any document unless you are completely certain about the outcome.

EIGHTH HOUSE: SHARED RESOURCES, BIRTH, DEATH, TAXES, THE OCCULT, SEX

There is fear and confusion regarding shared resources. Be cautious about entering any new financial arrangements with anyone until the confusion clears.

Death and the occult can be misconstrued as negative because of your fear.

A birth is a time of confusion.

Your sexual attitudes are riddled with fear and confusion.

NINTH HOUSE: PHILOSOPHY, SPIRITUALITY, HIGHER EDUCATION, LONG JOURNEYS

Your thinking is so muddy that you can't put matters of a spiritual or philosophical nature into perspective. Until you make up your mind about what you are seeking, you won't be able to take any steps forward.

Any travel under this influence would only add to your confusion. There would be no relaxation, enjoyment, or learning.

TENTH HOUSE: CAREER, FATHER (OR MOTHER)

The career path ahead is not clear. Do not make any decisions until you can gain some understanding.

Feelings about the indicated parent may be confused.

ELEVENTH HOUSE: FRIENDS, HOPES, DREAMS, GROUPS

You need to reevaluate your friendships and weed out the negative associations. Be aware of any questionable and confused plans of friends. Think before you join any groups.

Your hopes and dreams are not clear. You may not have any at this time.

TWELFTH HOUSE: THE UNCONSCIOUS, KARMA, SECRET ENEMIES, RESTRICTIONS, INSTITUTIONS

You have many mixed thoughts that only confuse the issue, making you compulsive. Know your limitations and abide by them.

Your karmic lessons are not presently clear. Roll again for a glimpse of the lessons you will face.

A mistake in judgment could attract secret enemies and result in negative consequences and legal implications, possibly involving incarceration.

There is no intensified grey.

WHITE

FIRST HOUSE: THE SELF

You will reach an understanding of whatever concerns you through a cool, unemotional approach.

SECOND HOUSE: MONEY

You should be reaching an understanding about your financial matters that satisfies you.

THIRD HOUSE: COMMUNICATIONS, SHORT JOURNEYS, BROTHERS, SISTERS

All communications should be short and to the point. Don't overreact to impossible requests.

A short vacation could clear your mind, preparing you for the work at hand.

Being an understanding soul, you are protective toward brothers and sisters, whether they are blood related or members of the universal family.

FOURTH HOUSE: HOME ENVIRONMENT, MOTHER (OR FATHER)

A cool, unemotional home environment enhances clear thinking. Take advantage of the relaxed environment to reach an understanding of your situation.

The indicated parent is understanding but uninvolved.

FIFTH HOUSE: CREATIVITY, LOVE AFFAIRS, CHILDREN

You have the ability to stand apart from yourself. This

allows you to fully comprehend your creative nature and how you can use it to your best advantage.

Concerning a love affair, an understanding will be reached. The ardor may cool, but you will be protected. You will need to express your feelings.

Regarding children, take time to understand their viewpoints.

SIXTH HOUSE: WORK, HEALTH

By stepping outside your problems and trying to understand all views, you can clear away much of the stress surrounding you in the workplace.

Regarding your health, there's clear sailing ahead.

SEVENTH HOUSE: MARRIAGE, BUSINESS PARTNERSHIPS, CONTRACTS

Small problems related to your marriage will clear up by taking time to understand your spouse. Any thoughts of divorce are likely to be cold, calculating, and unemotional.

Regarding a partnership or contract, take the time to reach an understanding that will be suitable to both of you.

EIGHTH HOUSE: SHARED RESOURCES, BIRTH, DEATH, TAXES, THE OCCULT, SEX

Regarding shared resources, it will be beneficial if you and your partner reach an understanding. Clearing the air promotes harmony.

A birth will be a time of understanding. Death may take on new meaning in the coming months. You may come to see it as a new beginning.

In occult matters, your understanding serves as a shield of protection. Once you understand something, your fear vanishes.

You see sex as a means of understanding. There is a level of detachment in your thoughts.

NINTH HOUSE: PHILOSOPHY, SPIRITUALITY, HIGHER EDUCATION, LONG JOURNEYS

You have reached the heights of understanding, a pinnacle few have achieved. Education serves as a doorway for your philosophical or spiritual growth.

Any journey that is stimulating will be worthwhile.

TENTH HOUSE: CAREER, FATHER (OR MOTHER)

Regarding your career, a bright future depends on your actions now. The way is illuminated for you. You may soon be in the spotlight, if you aren't already.

The indicated parent harbors a glimmer of understanding but stands apart.

ELEVENTH HOUSE: FRIENDS, HOPES, DREAMS, GROUPS

Friendships lead to understanding. Groups with common goals can create higher awareness.

When you maintain a bright outlook, your hopes and dreams are always met with some form of success.

TWELFTH HOUSE: THE UNCONSCIOUS, KARMA, SECRET ENEMIES, RESTRICTIONS, INSTITUTIONS

The light of understanding brightens your existence. Your karma is to look for ways to help others attain a similar understanding.

The only restrictions you face are brought on by a lack of understanding. In your case, there's little to stop you. Your inner light blinds any secret enemies.

You have the capabilities of cutting through the jargon and decorative facades of institutions to reach the heart of a matter.

There is no intensified white.

BLACK

FIRST HOUSE: THE SELF

You are extremely secretive, and you hide your emotions. You stand apart, allowing no one near you.

SECOND HOUSE: MONEY

All factors are not being revealed. Be guarded with your finances. This is not a time for excessive spending.

THIRD HOUSE: COMMUNICATIONS, SHORT JOURNEYS, BROTHERS, SISTERS

There is a barrier blocking communication. Your sense of privacy keeps you from making contacts.

Short, secretive trips are indicated.

Your relationships with brothers and sisters are strained.

FOURTH HOUSE: HOME, ENVIRONMENT, MOTHER (OR FATHER)

The home is your refuge, a hiding place.

The relationship with the mother (or father) leaves a lot to be desired.

FIFTH HOUSE: CREATIVITY, LOVE AFFAIRS, CHILDREN

Because you are so inhibited, all your creativity is withheld. Any creative talent would be a private one.

You are so guarded that any love relationship would be strained.

There is poor rapport with children.

SIXTH HOUSE: WORK, HEALTH

Information about work is not revealed at this time.

Whenever black appears in the area of health, there is need for an examination. You could be a closet eater, smoker, drinker, etc.

SEVENTH HOUSE: MARRIAGE, BUSINESS PARTNERSHIPS, CONTRACTS

You are an uncommunicative person, difficult in marriage and in partnerships, and impossible in divorce.

Any contract signed could bring hidden problems. This is definitely not a time to deal with contracts.

EIGHTH HOUSE: SHARED RESOURCES, BIRTH, DEATH, TAXES, THE OCCULT, SEX

Fear and anxiety and numerous hang-ups dominate this house. In matters of shared resources, there may be something hidden.

Your thoughts are riddled with anxiety about death and the occult because of your fear of the unknown. There is something unknown or hidden regarding a birth.

Your attitudes about sex are hidden, possibly perverse.

NINTH HOUSE: PHILOSOPHY, SPIRITUALITY, HIGHER EDUCATION, LONG JOURNEYS

Your philosophical and spiritual growth is hampered by fear and ignorance. You may be negatively oriented about higher education.

You use long journeys as an escape so you won't have to deal with matters at hand.

TENTH HOUSE: CAREER, FATHER (OR MOTHER)

Your hidden desires can be realized. You need to set goals, then take steps to achieve them. The choice is yours.

The relationship with the father (or mother) is strained; there is no base of understanding.

ELEVENTH HOUSE: FRIENDS, HOPES, DREAMS, GROUPS

Relationships are closed. Friends are secretive. Be careful with any group involvement at this time.

Your thinking is far too negative. You don't allow yourself to hope or dream for anything.

TWELFTH HOUSE: THE UNCONSCIOUS, KARMA, SECRET ENEMIES, RESTRICTIONS, INSTITUTIONS

Negative thinking and hidden thoughts make for very strange situations. Your karmic lesson is to seek understanding and step away from negative influences.

You will find that you restrict yourself by your own thinking.

Do not contemplate doing anything illegal. Secret enemies could be working against you. You could end up incarcerated.

There is no intensified black.

RAINBOW

FIRST HOUSE: THE SELF

You are versatile and adaptable, sunshine bright.

SECOND HOUSE: MONEY

Your finances are on an upswing. You see a trend and should act upon it. A pot of gold is a motivating factor.

THIRD HOUSE: COMMUNICATIONS, SHORT JOURNEYS, BROTHERS, SISTERS

You communicate so well that you become all things to all people.

Short trips suit you because you like the change of scenery. You adapt well and look for new experiences.

Brothers and sisters look up to you. They see you as versatile and bright.

FOURTH HOUSE: HOME, ENVIRONMENT, MOTHER (OR FATHER)

Anyplace you hang your hat is home. You are that adaptable.

The relationship with the indicated parent is changing—the parent may seem to be the child now in certain situations.

FIFTH HOUSE: CREATIVITY, LOVE AFFAIRS, CHILDREN

Your versatility is shown in your creativity. You lend your creativity to everything you do.

Your relationships could never be dull. You are a chameleon.

You love all children and meet them on their own level.

SIXTH HOUSE: WORK, HEALTH

Work for you is a rejuvenating tonic.

You have a healthy glow that comes from your positive outlook.

SEVENTH HOUSE: MARRIAGE, BUSINESS PARTNERSHIPS, CONTRACTS

As long as you have a partner who is interesting, you can thrive, whether in marriage or in business. If you find yourself suffocating or stifled, your thoughts will turn toward terminating the relationship.

Any contract you sign should leave room for flexibility.

EIGHTH HOUSE: SHARED RESOURCES, BIRTH, DEATH, TAXES, THE OCCULT, SEX

Joint resources should be helpful—once you adapt them to your particular needs.

Your openness and adaptability make your approach to the occult one of understanding. There is no fear of death, and great happiness regarding birth.

You greet sex with the joy of life. You're rarely bored by it, and are adaptable to new situations.

NINTH HOUSE: PHILOSOPHY, SPIRITUALITY, HIGHER EDUCATION, LONG JOURNEYS

You're open-minded, with a strong curiosity about spiritual or philosophical matters. If there is any opportunity for gaining further knowledge, you will seek it.

Long journeys with varied itineraries are on the horizon.

TENTH HOUSE: CAREER, FATHER (OR MOTHER)

An opportunity is ahead. Take advantage of it. You won't regret it.

Your father (or mother) has been a motivating factor in your life. His or her influence has been varied.

ELEVENTH HOUSE: FRIENDS, HOPES, DREAMS, GROUPS

You are surrounded by many and varied friends. They are available when you need them. You adapt easily to any group situation.

Your hopes and dreams are many, and have a good chance of being realized.

TWELFTH HOUSE: THE UNCONSCIOUS, KARMA, SECRET ENEMIES, RESTRICTIONS, INSTITUTIONS

The inner "you" is very motivated because of your adaptability.

The karmic lessons are your choice. They may be light or harsh, depending on your own understanding.

People may envy you.

Restriction is not a word in your vocabulary. You cannot tolerate confinement in any way.

In any interaction with institutions, your approach is that rules are made to be changed.

★ ★ ★

There is no intensified rainbow.

10
WHAT'S YOUR
PERSONAL COLOR?

Each of us has a favorite color that reflects something about our personalities. If it's blue, it indicates a person who seeks tranquillity and peace. Yellow is the favorite color of people who use their intellect well and see the bright side of life. You can ask friends what their favorite colors are and learn something about them.

You can also use the color cubes to ask about your personal color—the dominant aspect of your personality at a particular time. The cube you roll, in essence, will reflect the aspect of your personality that is significant in your expression of yourself at this time. Tomorrow or next week another color may dominate as your personal color.

You only need to roll one cube. The first response will be the most accurate one. Additional rolls will most likely contradict the first, as your unconscious mind reacts to your attempt to second-guess it. If you roll an intensified color, consider the attributes of both the normal hue and its intensified tone. Judge on your own which one most readily applies. For additional details about a particular color, refer back to the interpretations in Chapter 7.

PERSONAL COLOR INTERPRETATIONS

RED
A high-energy person. Someone with unlimited resources. Always on the move.

Intensified attributes: A high-strung, highly emotional person, prone to excessive stress.

ORANGE
A balanced personality. Someone who weighs logic with emotion. A positive thinker.

Intensified attributes: An imbalance in the personality.

YELLOW
The intellectual. Logic is all-important. Everything must be orderly. This person has a sunny personality, but is often picky.

Intensified attributes: Logical-minded to the point of being rigid.

GREEN
A changeable personality. A person who is always looking ahead, wanting to grow.

Intensified attributes: An emotional chameleon, flighty and fickle, envious, sometimes deceitful and duplicitous.

BLUE

A private person, a loner, a solitary personality who looks within. The peacekeeper.

Intensified attributes: A lonely, depressed person who keeps everything inside.

PURPLE

A person with an established way of thinking, who is bound by numerous rules and regulations. Habits from the past or religion may provide the guidelines this person seeks.

Intensified attributes: Someone with many self-imposed restrictions and limitations. A rigid and unyielding personality.

BROWN

This person is security conscious, earthy, with both feet on the ground. A stable person.

In the intensified hue: A self-centered, insecure person who is governed by materialism.

PINK

The eternal romantic, loving life, and conscious of his or her health and vitality.

Intensified attributes: Concerned about love and health, but from a pessimistic point of view. A "nothing-ever-seems-to work-out-right" mentality.

PEACH

Someone who is romantic but balanced. A warm, mellow personality. Upbeat.

VIOLET

Violet denotes a spiritually oriented person who is concerned with the higher order of things. This person has little interest in mechanical, mundane activities. He or she would rather "chart the stars."

GOLD

This is the color of the high achiever—a goal-setting person who is usually successful in all he or she undertakes.

SILVER

An intuitive personality, this individual must be careful not to build "castles in the air."

GREY

Confusion reigns. The true personality is bogged down by muddled thoughts. Roll again later for a clearer view.

BLACK

A hidden personality. Someone with something to hide. Don't pry.

WHITE

An understanding person. He or she looks deeply into all sides of a matter, yet remains uninvolved.

RAINBOW

A person who fluctuates from being a positive thinker to a negative one, but is nevertheless lucky. Someone who can adjust to almost any circumstance.

11
AURA ANALYSIS

FOR CENTURIES, SEERS AND psychics have described auras or coronas of swirling colors around people. Scientists first took an interest in the subject in the early nineteenth century, when research was undertaken to find a way to perceive and to measure the subtle electromagnetic field radiating from the human body. To avoid any of the mystical connotations, researchers variously called these emanations an "odic force," the "human atmosphere," and "L-fields." For decades, most of their findings were debunked or ignored. Anything related to auras or fields of energy around the body was derided as occult mumbo jumbo.

Today, however, there is clear evidence that the human body transmits its own electromagnetic field. Electroencephalographs (EEGs), for example, measure brain waves. Other instruments measure galvanic skin response, the electrical charge carried by the skin. Such instruments are used to find acupuncture points for medical treatments. Earlier in this century, a Russian couple named Kirlian developed a photographic method of viewing auras. Although the process has been repeatedly attacked by skeptical scientists, who claim the flares of light around objects in the photographs are simply light leaks, there remains a solid base of evidence for the validity of this technique. For example, the aura outlining the missing part of a torn leaf will show up in a Kirlian photograph. No light leaks would account for such a phenomenon, often referred to as the "phantom limb" effect.

Generally speaking, auras are described by psychics as a constantly moving mélange of color. The only time one color dominates for an extended period of time is when a person is ill, troubled, overly excited, or extremely angry. Yet one color appears to predominate for shorter periods, displaying the emotional state of the person at that particular time. Although invisible to most of us, that dominant color is readily perceived at an unconscious level.

This dominant color can be demonstrated through the use of the *Rainbow Oracle*. Since the link between individuals at an unconscious level is not altered by physical distance, it is possible to perceive an indication of the dominant color of the aura of someone who is not present.

The method of taking aura readings is similar to throwing a cube on your own personal color described in the previous chapter. However, with this method you can read others as well as yourself. If you know the individual, you should be able to resonate with the response, especially if you've recently seen or talked with the person.

Ideally, it would seem that two people throwing a cube to determine another individual's aura would each roll the same color. However, auric readings with color cubes are quite subjective. In other words, your impression of a person's aura is filtered through your own personality and perceptions. If a second person were to throw a cube on the same individual, yet another color might turn up, because the perception would be filtered through the second thrower's personality.

Try it for yourself, and see how accurate the impressions are.

AURA COLOR INTERPRETATIONS

RED

A great deal of energy is being expended by the individual. It's a time of high emotions and much activity.

Intensified red could signify that extreme stress may be taking its toll on the individual.

ORANGE

The individual is balancing matters of the mind and those of the emotions.

Intensified orange suggests there is something out of balance at the present time.

YELLOW

The intellect is dominant. Emotional matters have been pushed aside for the moment. Usually, the individual is following a positive train of thought.

In the intensified hue, it appears that the individual is facing an intellectual block of some sort.

GREEN

A feeling of rejuvenation and healing is presently being experienced. For instance, it could be equated to the feeling that accompanies completion of a physical workout.

Intensified green denotes that the individual could be feeling envious and planning something that will seem treacherous to someone else.

BLUE

A sense of peace and tranquillity surrounds the individual at the present time.

In the intensified hue, a feeling of loneliness or isolation surrounds the individual.

PURPLE

The individual may be handling a matter that deals with the past. It could be a repetition of something that he or she has previously done.

Intensified purple indicates the individual is feeling restricted or tied to a way of doing something that is no longer relevant.

PINK

A feeling of love or a sense of health and vitality infuses this person.

Intensified pink suggests the individual is feeling a lack of love or vitality.

BROWN

This individual is feeling stable, secure.

In the intensified hue, a craving for material wealth is on the person's mind.

★ ★ ★

The following colors have no intensification:

PEACH

A relaxed, mellow feeling prevails.

VIOLET

The individual has come in touch with his or her higher self. An uplifting feeling, a sense of wonder prevails.

GOLD

A sense of achievement or high awareness envelops the person.

SILVER

The individual is putting his or her intuition to use.

GREY

Confusion reigns.

WHITE

This person is seeking clarification, understanding, or protection. He or she may be pursuing a line of thinking much like a detective following clues.

BLACK

Something is wrong or hidden.

RAINBOW

The aura is in a state of perfect harmony. No single color predominates at the moment.

12
COLOR MEDITATION

ONCE YOU ARE FAMILIAR with the meaning of color and its intimate connection with the unconscious mind, it's easy to understand how the hues of the rainbow can serve as a way of focusing your meditation. Color meditations can assist in the development of the power of self-healing and serve as a means of overcoming negative beliefs and conditioning.

Before providing specific color meditations, it's worthwhile to take a brief look at color and its relationship to the modern medical profession. For most of this century, physicians have shunned color therapies. The primary reason for this was that, near the turn of the twentieth century, color therapy was a favorite tool of charlatan healers who sold "Chromo Disks," "Chromo Flasks," and other gadgets for color treatments.

In recent years, however, there has been a renewed interest in the relationship between color and healing. For instance, infrared radiation has been found useful in relieving some types of pain, and ultraviolet light rays have also been used for physical therapy. In the visible light spectrum, baths of light emitting a high concentration of blue wavelengths are now used in many hospitals to cure infants of neonatal jaundice. The light penetrates the skin and breaks down the chemical bilirubin, which causes the condition. One of the treatments for herpes involves painting the affected area with dye and exposing it to visible light rays.

While the healing properties of colors are currently being recognized by the medical profession, you can also experiment with color in self-healing exercises. The first step is to select the color you wish to use. Read over the significance of the colors listed below, and select one.

MEDITATIVE USES OF COLOR

RED

This color ray comes from the warm side of the spectrum, and helps stimulate and vitalize. It can be used to bolster strength, courage, and enthusiasm. Meditation with red may also be used to help improve the body's circulation, and to counter depression. However, you should be cautious when using red. Concentrated meditation on the color in experiments has resulted in the release of adrenaline, has increased the amount of hemoglobin in the blood, and has even raised body temperature.

ORANGE

Use orange to attain balance between the mind and the emotions. If you feel as if you are being pulled in two directions on a matter—one way by your emotions and another by your logical mind—orange would be a good choice for meditation on the concern. It can also work to counter depression, and feelings of limitation and restriction. While orange is a color of balance and positive thinking, like red, it can also result in overstimulation: Use it with care.

YELLOW

This is the color of the mind, a ray that is particularly effective for clarifying thoughts. As such, it is a color that can be used for processing ideas and concepts. For example, if you feel inundated by ideas and their possibilities and can't make a decision, yellow would be a worthwhile color to use to help you reach a conclusion.

GREEN

This ray, located in the middle of the spectrum between the warm and cool colors, is useful for meditation when you wish to make a change of some sort. It is also helpful for promoting growth and for renewing health.

BLUE

A soothing color, blue is helpful for relaxing and easing "frayed" nerves. It is also a useful color for looking within— for raising one's awareness. It is, in essence, the color of meditation, of devotional endeavors, of peace, tranquility, and harmony. It is helpful in meditation for combating insomnia.

PURPLE

A highly philosophical or religious color, purple denotes restrictions or self-discipline within the philosophy. It is a ray that is useful for self-discipline and control over the emotions; it also helps in recalling the past. Purple is a cool red or a warm blue. It can be used in meditation for controlling pain.

PINK

The focus of this hue is love and vitality. Pink is the color to use when seeking a new love, or healing a broken heart. It is a color of healing and renewed youth, of regeneration. It is also a color for experimenting with a "meditative face-lift." Flood the skin cells of your face and body with the color and concentrate on revitalization.

BROWN

A color that in some ways may seem contradictory to the process of meditation, brown is nonetheless useful for helping you get down to the basics of a matter. It is a color to focus on when you are concerned about security, or feel you are losing your grip on a matter. It helps you put down roots.

PEACH

This is a color of harmony. If a friendship or romance has become strained, meditate on peach as a means of attracting balance and love to the situation.

VIOLET

A color of inspiration, of spiritual growth, violet is the key ray for understanding the higher purpose of life. It is a color most useful for those seeking understanding of the higher planes of existence.

GOLD

This hue can be used to help bring about the achievement of your goals. Meditation with the color should be accompanied by specific thoughts of what you are seeking to accomplish. The color can also be used in its alchemical sense as a tool of transformation. You can meditate on the color with the intent of personal transformation to a higher state.

SILVER

The color of mercury, silver helps in developing intuition or opening psychic channels. Keep an open mind and allow the flow of the color to provide information that is significant.

WHITE

Focusing on white helps to clear the mind and the emotions in order to chase away gloom and despair. Surrounding yourself with white light evokes understanding, wisdom, and truth, and as a result helps you provide your own protection.

RAINBOW

When focusing on the spectrum of the rainbow, accompany your visualizing with the idea that the colors you need will flood your being. Which colors are they? Look up their meanings. Later, focus on those individual colors during meditations.

Black and grey are not included as colors for meditation. Little can be gained from focusing one's attention on what is not being revealed (black) or confusion (grey).

THE MEDITATIONS

Now, find a place where you won't be disturbed. Display the color you are planning to use in your meditation. You might place a colored light bulb in a lamp, and shut off all other light sources. You could also wear an article of clothing with the color, or place an object of that color before you.

Loosen any tight garments that might hamper you from becoming relaxed. Sit down on a comfortable chair or on a cushion. It's best to remain sitting, instead of lying down, so you won't fall asleep.

Now you're ready. Read over the meditations. You can use them as they are or, if you already use a method of meditation, you can adapt these to fit your own method.

The purpose of this meditation is to use the color you have chosen to energize, uplift, and heal. Begin by breathing deeply to the count of five. Hold your breath for another five counts, then exhale to the count of five. Repeat the pattern several times. As you breathe, think of your body relaxing. Start with your toes and work your way up to the top of your head.

When you feel totally relaxed and at ease, imagine a balloon in the color you have chosen. The balloon represents you. Now picture it expanding. Watch it closely and focus on the color. If you see another color instead of the one you chose, go with it. It may be the color you need at this time.

When you feel the balloon has gotten as big as it should be, practice making it smaller, then larger, then smaller again. This is a way of allowing yourself to gain control over the images you are experiencing. If the balloon won't do what you want, keep practicing. But don't worry about it—remind yourself that you are in control, and nothing will interfere with your imaging. (Once you can easily manipulate the size of the balloon, you can skip this part of the meditation.)

Now, allow the balloon to float slowly upward. Feel the freedom as it floats higher and higher. You are there with the balloon. You are the balloon—nothing can harm you. You can look down from the perspective of the balloon. You may see clearly, or you might just get a sense of things below you.

You pass through clouds and as you do, try to feel their texture. They are soft, moist, billowy. Pick one out to settle on. Allow yourself to float on it. Think of the sun above you, the brightness and the warmth. Feel your color become even richer and more energized. You become one with your chosen color.

After a while, feel yourself descending slowly until you see your own body. Allow yourself to enter your body from the top of your head. As you do, you will feel the colored rays of energy moving through you like a stream—down through the top of your head, your neck, shoulders, arms, hands, chest, waist, hips, thighs, calves, and feet.

Now feel the flow of energy reverse direction. As it moves up, you might find that it feels more intense in some areas of your body. Imagine that part of you absorbing the color, being healed and revitalized. When the intensity lessens, follow the flow of energy as it continues its slow progress up through your body. Does it concentrate in another area? If so, repeat the healing process.

After the energy has completely passed through you, clear your mind and relax yourself. Feel the color continue to circulate about your body. It is pure, clear, and energizing. It awakens your body, lifts your spirits, and fills you with a positive feeling.

Open your eyes. You are back.

To simplify things, make a tape of this meditation, starting with the breathing exercise. You can do the same for the following meditation.

CHAKRA MEDITATION

In using color meditation for self-healing, it's helpful to understand the concept of chakras. These are seven cosmic centers, or vortices of energy, each associated with a particular area of the body and a color of the spectrum of the rainbow. Chakras have been a part of Eastern metaphysical thought and practices for thousands of years. The word itself is of Hindu origin and means "wheel of fire."

Even if you know little about chakras and have never felt or sensed this energy, you can undertake a chakra meditation and experience the benefits for yourself. Here are the locations of the chakras and the colors associated with them.

Chakra 1—RED. Located at the base of the spine.
Chakra 2—ORANGE. In the area of the spleen,
about two inches below the navel.
Chakra 3—YELLOW. The solar plexus.
Chakra 4—GREEN. The heart.
Chakra 5—BLUE. The throat.
Chakra 6—INDIGO. Pineal gland—the "third eye,"
located between the eyebrows.
Chakra 7—VIOLET. Pituitary gland, located
at the top of the skull at the fontanelles.

The following meditation using the chakras and their colors is intended to relax, revitalize, and uplift.

Make yourself comfortable, and begin breathing deeply to the five counts described in the previous meditation. Relax your muscles from head to foot. When you are completely at ease, feel your body becoming lighter, almost weightless.

Now, picture a pure white glowing light directly in front of you. Concentrate on drawing the energy from this brilliant light into your body. Starting at your feet, feel it move slowly upward. As it moves up your legs, it turns to a pinkish color. When it reaches your upper thighs, it becomes a glowing red.

Picture a flower bud at the lower end of your spine. Focus the red light on the flower, making it open petal by petal until it is in full bloom. Become aware of the warmth and tingling in your lower body.

Move the light upward, watching it turn from red to orange as it centers in your umbilical area. In this area, once again picture the bud of a flower. Now open it with the orange energy force. When the flower is completely open and you feel the warmth, move the light upward to the solar plexus. There it turns to a bright yellow, like sunshine. Image another flower bud and watch it open. Drink in the sensations as it blossoms.

Continue moving the light slowly upward. It turns from yellow to green as it reaches the area of the heart. Imagine the flower bud opening within the light. When you feel a sense of vitality, draw the light upward.

Watch as it turns to a pale blue by the time it reaches the throat area. Visualize the bud again. Open it, and feel the results. Any constriction in the throat is released. You are relaxed and at peace.

Now the light rises to the center of the forehead, where it becomes a deep indigo blue, and another bud blossoms in the intense light. Watch it open, petal by petal, and feel a tingling. In the center of the flower, imagine a closed eye. See this eye open. As it does, become aware of the brightness and clarity of the energy.

Finally, envision the light moving to the top of the head, changing to violet. Picture the bud of a flower once again, and watch each petal slowly open. As it does, you realize your entire body is enveloped in a luminous egg.

Now, feel yourself rising, passing through the ceiling and the roof, floating upward through the clouds. Picture a large golden door in front of you. The door is sectioned in panels, and on each one is a painting. Step closer to the door and examine the panels. Each one is a mandala, a symbol of wholeness. Reach out and touch them. As you are doing this, the door slowly opens and you enter.

You see a vast, bright space before you. And as you adjust to the brightness, you become aware of a benevolent presence. Feel the love radiating from this being. You might think of this entity as a guide, an evolved master, or your Higher Self. Reach out, let the love enfold you.

Now see this presence in human form. Gaze into the being's eyes. Feel the sense of heightened awareness and joy. After a few minutes, thank the entity for all that you have experienced.

Finally, return slowly, taking with you an uplifting sense of well-being. You are totally relaxed, revitalized, and at one with your surroundings. Open your eyes. You are back.

13
THE POT OF GOLD

UNDERSTANDING THE deeper meaning of color and putting this knowledge to use in your daily life is one of many ways of expanding your awareness. Like any goal worth attaining, it takes practice and concentration. You may experience a burst of intuitive awareness at the outset, or it may be a gradual building process, a slow development of that awareness. Whichever way it develops, you are placing yourself in contact with the magical side of existence.

The magic of the *Rainbow Oracle* is that the answers to your questions are already within you. All we see and feel and experience comes from within. In essence, the mind is the source of our reality.

Defenders of our rational, scientific tradition may respond that oracles appear to provide correct answers because the responses are so general that they fit almost any situation. Those critics also contend that people who consult cards, stones, or shells, or the *Rainbow Oracle* are usually befuddled types who can't think for themselves.

Yet it's increasingly evident that more and more people who are firmly grounded in their thinking and successful in their lives are quietly becoming aware that the wonders of the mind extend beyond the limitations dictated by rational thought. And, in this respect, they are accepting what they can experience, even if they can't prove it beyond a doubt to anyone else. As Einstein once said, "The most beautiful and most profound emotion we can experience is the sensation of the mystical. It is the sower of all true science."

At the beginning of this century, mystics taught that the colors of the rainbow symbolize the levels of human spiritual evolution from the base material to the planes of higher awareness. Since humans first appeared on Earth, we have passed through the red, orange, and yellow rays, and are now on the verge of passing out of the green ray, located in the center of the spectrum. In other words, we have experienced the lower periods of material existence and are heading toward the higher ages of spiritual enlightenment. We are, in fact, on the verge of experiencing the higher vibration of the blue ray. Such a shift, however, is not without its difficulties, and we are already experiencing some of the trials—famine, drought, environmental decay, and plaguelike diseases—as the earth enters a new era.

Yet, as physicist F. David Peat has written: "Once we realize that our consciousness is without limit, then it becomes possible for us to engage in a creative transformation of our own lives and of the society we live in. From this perspective, we will have no more need for tortoiseshells and milfoil stalks, for we will have learned to live with the wisdom and understanding that has been present in us since the dawn of humanity."

What's taking place amid the chaos of world events is

known as a "paradigm shift." At a certain point, enough people will accept that reality exists beyond the physical, that consciousness is the source of the physical world rather than the other way around, and that we all have the ability to communicate and draw positive power to our lives from those invisible realms. Then, the old paradigm will dissolve, and a new one will take its place. The blue ray signals the end of the bitter struggles, and the advent of the time of the spiritual warrior.

As Chogyam Trungpa, author of *Shambhala: The Sacred Path of the Warrior*, put it: "We can appreciate the best of this world. We can appreciate its vividness: the yellowness of yellow, the redness of red, the greenness of green, the purpleness of purple. . . . Our experience is real. And when we appreciate reality, it can actually work for us."

The rainbow is arcing over us, and the pot of gold awaits our arrival. The gleaming nuggets within represent our successful transformation, the point when we will finally realize that all humankind is one, that higher awareness is our true birthright, and that we are ready to move a step closer to All That Is, the source from which we all spring.

APPENDIX A
CORRESPONDENCES

Quantum physics theorizes that everything in the universe is interconnected. The same theory can be applied to various systems of divination. Although each divinatory system is unique, there are correspondences between them. Thus, the colors of the *Rainbow Oracle* can be related to astrological signs, Runes, the *I Ching*, and the Egyptian Cartouche and Tarot cards.

In all likelihood, these systems developed independently. In other words, one did not necessarily spring from another. Instead, the correspondences suggest that the source of all the systems is the collective unconscious of humanity, which—if you like—can be thought of as our link with the divine.

For those familiar with other methods of divination, the following correspondences between the *Rainbow Oracle* and each divinatory method should provide added meaning. Although our system of correspondences is still a "work in progress," these are the initial similarities that have meaning to us. We invite you to experiment with them, and to write and let us know your results.

THE TAROT AND THE CARTOUCHE

Here, the colors of the *Rainbow Oracle* are coordinated with the cards from the higher arcana of the Tarot and the deck of the Egyptian Cartouche. In this case, the meanings of the colors as described here correspond to the meanings of the card symbols. The (I) designation after colors refers to their intensified hues, and corresponds with the reversal of some of the Cartouche cards. Since the meaning of the individual elements of all three systems is a subjective matter, other associations could be made. Because of the variables, no one set of correspondences is necessarily the *right* one.

COLOR/TAROT/CARTOUCHE CORRESPONDENCES

COLOR	TAROT	CARTOUCHE
Red	Strength	Ankh
Red (I)	The Chariot	Fire (Reversed)
Orange	Justice	Osiris
Orange (I)	The Hanged Man	Set
Yellow	The Emperor	Thoth
Yellow (I)	The Moon	Air (Reversed)
Green	The Empress	Hathor/Buckle of Isis
Green (I)	The Devil	Set (Reversed)
Blue	Judgment	Lotus
Blue (I)	The Hermit	Lotus (Reversed)
Purple	The Hierophant	Horus
Purple (I)	The Fool	Anubis (Reversed)
Pink	The Lovers	The Twins
Brown	Wheel of Fortune	Earth
Brown (I)	The Tower	Crook and Flail (Reversed)
Peach	The Sun	Scarab
Violet	Temperance	Pyramid
Gold	The World	Winged Disk
Silver	High Priestess/Star	Isis/Bast
Grey	The Magician	Uraeus
Black	Death	Sphinx
White	The Star	Sirius

THE RUNES

Here again, correspondences can be made matching aspects of the Runes with the nature of the colors. In general, the intensified color corresponds with the related Rune in its reversed position. In other words, intensified red is the Warrior reversed.

In several instances, more than one Rune is associated with a color. Aspects of those Runes resonate with the color. However, no one Rune completely corresponds with a color. As with all correspondences, the selections are highly subjective.

COLOR/RUNE/CORRESPONDENCES

COLOR	RUNE	SYMBOL
Red	Warrior	ᛏ
Orange	Wholeness/Journey	ᛊ ᚱ
Yellow	Protection	ᛉ
Green	Fertility/Growth	ᛝ ᛒ
Blue	Self/Defense/Gateway	ᛗ ᛇ ᚦ
Purple	Constraint	ᚾ
Pink	Partnership	ᚷ
Brown	Possessions/Retreat	ᚠ ᛟ
Peach	Joy	ᚹ
Violet	Breakthrough	ᛞ
Gold	Harvest	ᛃ
Silver	Flow/Movement/Signals	ᛚ ᛖ ᚨ
Grey	Standstill	ᛁ
White	Openings	ᚲ
Black	Initiation	ᛈ
Rainbow	The Unknowable	□

THE I CHING

In the left-hand column are the eight basic trigrams of the *I Ching*. In the center are the names of the trigrams, and in the right-hand column are the colors associated with each of them. While it's interesting to note that the Chinese associated a color with each trigram, it should be pointed out that the attributes of the trigram are not necessarily the same as those associated with the colors of the *Rainbow Oracle*. The Chinese also defy our Western assumptions about the colors of the elements. Note that Water/The Deep is red and Fire/Sun is yellow.

COLOR/TRIGRAM CORRESPONDENCES

☰	Heaven	Purple
☷	Earth	Black
☳	Thunder	Orange
☵	Water/The Deep	Red
☶	Mountain	Green
☴	Wind/Wood	White
☲	Fire/Sun	Yellow
☱	Lake/Mist	Blue

ASTROLOGICAL SIGNS AND COLOR

The following are correspondences of astrological signs and colors. However, it should be noted that the meanings of the colors as described in the *Rainbow Oracle* do not necessarily agree with the nature of the signs.

COLOR/ASTROLOGY CORRESPONDENCES

Aries	Red
Taurus	Red-orange
Gemini	Orange
Cancer	Orange-yellow
Leo	Yellow
Virgo	Yellow-green
Libra	Green
Scorpio	Green-blue
Sagittarius	Blue
Capricorn	Blue-violet
Aquarius	Violet
Pisces	Violet-red

COLOR AND MUSIC

"Tone," "pitch," "intensity," "color," and "chromatic" are words used in both art and music. In a sense, you can "see" music through color. According to Corinne Heline, author of *Color and Music in the New Age*, when Franz Liszt was composing his symphonies, he used phrases such as, "More pink here." "This is too black." "I want it all azure." Beethoven called B minor the black key. Schubert likened E minor "unto a maiden robed in white and with a rose-red bow on her breast."

The following comment by Christopher Ward was cited in Faber Birren's *Color Psychology and Color Therapy*. It's a wonderfully poetic description of the connection between color and music. "From the faintest murmur of pearl-gray, through the fluttering of blue, the oboe note of violet, the cool, clear wood-wind of green, the mellow piping of yellow, the bass of brown, the bugle-call of scarlet, the sounding brass of orange, the colors are music."

Many composers have made associations between color and music. In the following arrangement of sound and color, notice that the three fundamental notes of the musical scale—the first, third, and fifth—correspond with the three primary colors—red, yellow, and blue.

SOUND/COLOR CORRESPONDENCES

Do	Red
Re	Orange
Mi	Yellow
Fa	Green
Sol	Blue
La	Purple
Ti	Violet
Do	Red (higher octave)

The Russian composer Aleksandr Scriabin attempted to correlate musical notes to color. In his *Prometheus*, he developed a part for a color organ, which he called "Luce." Here is how Scriabin related color to the notes in the diatonic scale:

SCRIABIN'S SOUND/COLOR CORRESPONDENCES

C	Red
C#	Violet
D	Yellow
D#	Silver
E	Pearly blue
F	Dark red
F#	Bright blue
G	Rosy orange
G#	Purple
A	Green
A#	Silver
B	Soft blue

APPENDIX B
OTHER USES OF COLOR

THERE ARE NUMEROUS other ways to use the color cubes. We've included a few alternate methods you might try. Once you've become familiar with the meanings of the colors through frequent use, you can experiment with your own methods.

COLOR OF THE DAY

Roll a cube at the beginning of your day. Then take a moment and meditate on its meaning and how it might apply to your day. You might choose clothing with this color, or you might count the number of times you notice the color during the day. Let the message of the color guide you.

If you don't like the color that turns up, use it simply as a caution. Any color you roll is merely a reflection of your unconscious state of mind. Be aware of the possible nature of your day and make an effort to alter the situation to one that you find more appealing. Be positive. See the change that you want. Act it out in your mind using examples of what might take place. Then let it go, and be confident that it will happen as you wish.

Here are the color interpretations that will help you answer the question: What will my day be like?

DAILY COLORS

RED

A fast-paced, high-energy day is in store. You may face stressful circumstances and have to control your emotions.

ORANGE

This is a day to stay balanced. Carefully weigh and measure all that you do.

YELLOW

Pay attention to details today. A day of intellect and logic is ahead.

GREEN

Expect a day of change. There may be new beginnings, or the growth of something you've recently started.

BLUE

A quiet, peaceful day is ahead. There will be no highs or lows.

PURPLE

A day of limitations is likely. Be sensitive to the rules and regulations you face.

PINK

A high-vitality day is in store. Conditions are ripe for loving exchanges.

BROWN

It will be a good day for planting seeds, for letting projects take root. There could be material gain, foundations built.

PEACH

Prepare yourself for a good day. You can accomplish much. It's an excellent day to charm or influence someone.

VIOLET

The day may bring you in touch with a higher order of awareness. Your thoughts may hit new highs. One caution: Don't get caught with your head in the clouds.

GOLD

If you're setting out today with a goal in mind, chances are you'll achieve it. A lucrative day is in the offing.

SILVER

Use your intuition. Follow your gut reactions today.

GREY

Your outlook is confused. Throw again for clarification.

WHITE

You'll reach a clear understanding today regarding a matter on your mind.

BLACK

Something will be hidden today. There could be surprises. Consider changing your plans to counter unwanted events.

RAINBOW

A multifaceted day is ahead. Enjoy the variety of action today. Keep your sunny side up.

PERSONALITY READINGS

An interesting experiment involves throwing a cube on a well-known person and seeing how accurately your beliefs about the individual's personality fit with the interpretation for the color. To some extent, the color will reveal the way you think about the person as well as who that person actually is. If someone else throws a cube on the same person, they'll be seeing the individual through their own perceptions.

Here are several examples thrown for this purpose. Try some on your own.

RONALD REAGAN: ORANGE

A balanced personality who weighs logic with emotion. A positive thinker.

Whether you share former President Reagan's political philosophy or policies or find them repugnant, it is widely felt that he is a positive thinker. Even when the stock market crashed in October 1987, losing 500 points in a single day, he was smiling and saying that the economy was sound. Two days later when the market started to rally, he optimistically boasted that the worst was over

It also can be argued that President Reagan weighs logic with emotion. The nuclear arms issue is a case in point. His logic called for a strong defense. However, when the dangers of a continued nuclear buildup became an emotional issue, he attempted to balance the two aspects by meeting with the Soviets for serious talks on nuclear arms reduction.

When President Reagan slipped out of balance between

emotions and logic, he tumbled into trouble. That was the case with the Iran-Contra arms scandal. His high emotional interest in freeing American captives in the Mideast and his strong allegiance to the Contras led him into approval, tacit or otherwise, of actions that later embarrassed his administration. Had he balanced logic with emotions, as he had so often done, some of the more flagrant dealings of his advisors probably would not have taken place.

MUAMMAR QADHAFI: ORANGE (Intensified)

Irrational thought. Imbalance. A pessimist.

Qadhafi is a man who acts on imbalanced emotions, whose power is based on his ability to emotionally rally support against his adversaries. He focuses on the negative, the "American devils" who must be defeated.

PRINCESS DIANA: GREEN

A changeable personality, always wanting to grow, attracted to new ideas.

At the time the cube was thrown, Princess Diana and Prince Charles had been apart for several weeks, and there was considerable speculation about the stability of their relationship. There was evidence that, indeed, Diana was a changeable personality, who might be thinking that royalty and tradition, linked with the past, were preventing her from fulfilling her own individual needs.

JOHNNY CARSON: PEACH

Romantic but balanced. A warm, mellow personality. Upbeat.

The talk show entertainer's romances, wives, and divorces have been well publicized. Carson, in fact, uses his romantic ups and downs as comedy material, suggesting an ability to maintain balance. His warm, witty, upbeat personality has spanned decades of public exposure.

ARNOLD SCHWARZENEGGER: BROWN

Security-conscious, earthy, with two feet on the ground. A stable person.

The bodybuilder and actor personifies the idea of an earthy person. Born and raised in Austria, he came to the United States to seek fame and fortune. He has said there was little opportunity for someone like him to gain stature and wealth in his native country. In the U.S., he has embraced the American dream and found the security he sought.

HOROSCOPE VARIATIONS

You may also want to experiment with the alternate horoscope method. There are several variations you can try. You can ask a specific question, and throw the colors for the twelve houses. You can also focus on a particular month. For example, you might ask: "What's my outlook for the month of June?" and throw for the twelve houses.

Another interesting variation involves tossing the cubes on a circular horoscope layout. This method requires a little preparation in that you need to draw a horoscope layout on a sheet of paper. Once that's done, simply ask your question, and drop all the cubes at once on the chart, letting them literally roll where they may. You then read the colors according to the house. Alternately, you can roll one cube at a time.

These variations are ideas for experimentation once you've familiarized yourself with the other methods and the meanings of the colors. You should be aware that when you ask specific questions with a horoscope method, the interpretations for the houses may need to be adjusted in orientation. Since the interpretations focus on a personality readout, a question about a career change, for example, would require you to shift the interpretation to a material orientation.

GROUP DECISIONS

Perhaps you work in an environment where innovative ways of gaining perspective or advancing ideas are encouraged. If that's the case, the color cubes could be an ideal working tool to introduce to the *right* people at the right time.

Say there's a project on the table that could be pursued in two different ways. There are advocates of each method, and others who are undecided. If you've had some experience with the cubes privately and have found them to be insightful, you might suggest rolling the color cubes on the matter.

Tell everyone to set aside rational thinking for a moment and rely on intuition instead. For example, you could throw a six-cube spread for a prognosis on each of the methods under discussion. Stress that it's simply a way of gaining a fresh perspective, and no one will be committed to accepting the interpretations. Let everyone participate by throwing a cube.

Don't expect everyone to take the cubes seriously, especially on the first try. But time will tell. Next week or next month, when the results are in, look back at the reading. How accurate was it? Make mention of it to your colleagues. See how they respond. Don't be surprised if some call it luck or nonsense. You may want to return to the "closet" with your cubes. On the other hand, you may have won new advocates for the magic of the oracle.

LET US KNOW

The authors would like to hear about your experiences with the *Rainbow Oracle*. We're especially interested in hearing from people who have put it to innovative uses. You can write the authors c/o Ballantine Books, 201 E. 50th St.—9th Floor, New York, New York 10022.